MW01106046

Mastering SQL Server 2014 Data Mining

Master selecting, applying, and deploying data mining models to build powerful predictive analysis frameworks

Amarpreet Singh Bassan

Debarchan Sarkar

[PACKT] enterprise
PUBLISHING professional expertise distilled

BIRMINGHAM - MUMBAI

Mastering SQL Server 2014 Data Mining

First published: December 2014

Production reference: 1221214

Published by Packt Publishing Ltd.
Livery Place
35 Livery Street
Birmingham B3 2PB, UK.

ISBN 978-1-84968-894-9

www.packtpub.com

Credits

About the Authors

Amarpreet Singh Bassan is a Microsoft Data Platform engineer who works on SQL Server and its surrounding technologies. He is a subject matter expert in SQL Server Analysis Services and reporting services. Amarpreet is also a part of Microsoft's HDInsight team.

> I sincerely wish to thank the entire Packt Publishing team, especially Greg and Arvind. I would like to thank my co-author, Debarchan Sarkar, whom I fondly call "dada" for giving me the opportunity to write this book. I dedicate this title to my family for their encouragement and support to make this endeavor successful.

Debarchan Sarkar is a Microsoft Data Platform engineer. He specializes in the Microsoft SQL Server Business Intelligence stack. Debarchan is a subject matter expert in SQL Server Integration Services and delves deep into the open source world, specifically the Apache Hadoop framework. He is currently working on a technology called HDInsight, which is Microsoft's distribution of Hadoop on Windows. He has authored various books on SQL Server and Big Data, including *Microsoft SQL Server 2012 with Hadoop, Packt Publishing*, and *Pro Microsoft HDInsight: Hadoop on Windows, Apress*. His Twitter handle is `@debarchans`.

I wish to thank Amarpreet for the tremendous effort that he has put into this title. I was just an enabler; the bulk of the credit goes to him. I would also like to thank the entire Packt Publishing team for their patience throughout and the technical reviewers for their insightful reviews.

I wish to acknowledge the help and support provided by my parents, Devjani Sarkar and Asok Sarkar; without their love and encouragement, this book wouldn't have become a reality.

I want to dedicate this book to my wife, Ankita Ghosh. I know that our journey together has just begun. I'm sure that we are going to enjoy this journey to its fullest until our last breath. The future might be made up of many factors, but it truly lies in our hearts and minds. Thanks for being there with me!

About the Reviewers

Tony Dong is a software engineer with focus on distributed systems, data infrastructure, and system architecture. He is currently a platform engineer at TellApart—a predictive marketing platform that allows merchants to target shoppers in an effective way. Tony graduated with distinction from the Honors Computer Engineering Program at the University of Waterloo.

Garrett Edmondson is an independent data science consultant with over 10 years of experience focused on delivering valuable business-oriented intellectual property in the form of data integration and data models for data mining and advanced analytical solutions based on Machine Learning. As a Solutions Architect and developer, he is responsible for all the phases of the software development life cycle.

Juan Carlos González has almost 11 years of experience in the ICT sector. The best thing that defines Juan Carlos in terms of technology is his interest and knowledge of new technologies, which comes to him naturally in terms of attending and solving customers' problems and needs. Juan Carlos' career in the TIC sector, particularly in the .NET platform, started in 2003, just after he finished his studies at the university in the global worldwide consultancy company, Accenture. There, he had the opportunity to work for 3 years on big national and international projects performing different tasks and roles, such as the development of VB.NET applications, application test and deployment, management of small development teams, and so on. In May 2006, he quit Accenture and started a new adventure at the Microsoft Innovation Center in Cantabria (CIIN) as a Solutions Architect. At this new stage, he had the opportunity to gain in-depth knowledge about a variety of Microsoft technologies, such as SharePoint, Office 365, Windows Azure, Visual Studio, SQL Server, BizTalk Server, LINQ, Entity Framework, and so on. At CIIN, Juan Carlos performed several evangelism activities just around these technologies. He had the honor of belonging to one of the more specialized organizations in SharePoint in Spain.

In October 2013, Juan Carlos joined LKS as a consultant and Solutions Architect, skilled in SharePoint and Office 365 platforms. His daily work in LKS is focused on providing SharePoint and Office 365 advice and consultancy. He is also specialized in training and evangelism with regards to the different projects and LKS customers that he is involved with.

Juan Carlos is a SharePoint Server MVP since 2008. He is also a coordinator of the Cantabria .NET Users Group (Nuberos.NET, `http://www.nuberos.es/`). Apart from this, Juan Carlos is the co-founder and coordinator of the technology users groups, namely, the SharePoint Users Group of Spain (SUGES, `http://www.suges.es/Paginas/Home.aspx`), the Cloud Computing Users Group, and the Comunidad de Office 365. He is also the coeditor and director of the free Spanish digital magazine dedicated to SharePoint: CompartiMOSS (`http://www.compartimoss.com/`). Juan Carlos has co-authored four books and several articles on the SharePoint platform in Spanish and English.

Goh Yong Hwee is a database specialist, systems engineer, developer, and trainer based in Singapore. He is a Microsoft Certified Trainer and Certified Novell Instructor. Some of the courses that he is authorized to deliver and has delivered include Microsoft SQL Server Business Intelligence, Microsoft Windows Server, Microsoft SharePoint, Microsoft Exchange Server, and Suse Linux Enterprise Server. Throughout his trainings, he has consistently maintained a "Metrics that Matter" score exceeding 8 out of 10. He has also been instrumental in customizing and reviewing his training center's trainings for its clients. In imparting knowledge, his objective has been making technologies easy and simple for everyone to learn. His no-frills approach towards training has gained him recognitions over the years from both clients and employers, and his clinching of the Best Instructor Award, an accolade conferred by his employer, bears testimony to this fact. He has been in the training industry for 5 years at the time of writing this book and prior to that, he was attached to a Japanese MNC in Singapore as a Systems Analyst specialized in data warehousing on Microsoft SQL Server and RPG programming on the IBM iSeries and BPCS ERP. Over the years, he has chosen to focus his work and specialization on Microsoft SQL Server and is currently in full-time employment with a Fortune 500 company in Singapore—taking up specialist, consultancy, developer, and management roles.

David Loo is a senior software development professional with over 25 years of experience in both software development and people management. He is respected for his ability to motivate his teams to focus on service excellence and design and implement practical process improvements and solutions. David is always on the lookout for ways to contribute his knowledge and experience in the field of software development, team-building, and development best practices.

Richard Louie is a senior Business Intelligence professional with over 20 years of experience in software development and project management. He has extensive hands-on experience in Oracle and Microsoft SQL for ETL, SSIS, SSRS, SSAS, and VB.Net. He has architected and implemented data warehouses in the technological industry. A life-long learner, Richard is a graduate from the University of California, Irvine, in Information and Computer Science and is ASQ Green Belt certified. He has reviewed *Getting Started with SQL Server 2012 Cube Development*, *Getting Started with SQL Server 2014 Administration*, *SQL Server 2014 Development Essentials*, all by Packt Publishing.

Sivakumar Vellingiri is a Solutions Architect for Business Intelligence & Data Platforms at Wenso Solutions, United Kingdom. During his illustrious career spanning more than 12 years, Sivakumar has been instrumental in giving expertise solutions for Business Intelligence, data architecture, and development of various projects in the domain of BI and Database technologies using MS SQL Server, Oracle, and various database platforms. He has acquired extensive hands-on experience in data mining, data warehousing, and database design, and development by utilizing high-end techniques and best practices to tune and optimize high transaction database systems.

Sivakumar is a Microsoft Certified Solutions Expert in Business Intelligence and Data Platform. He is also certified in International Knowledge Measurement (IKM) for Business Intelligence. Sivakumar shares his knowledge and voices his opinions through his blogs, `http://sqlvoice.com/` and `http://sivasqlbi.blogspot.in/`, on various subjects concerning SQL Server and Business Intelligence technologies. He has reviewed *SQL Server 2012 Reporting Services Blueprints, Packt Publishing*. In future, Sivakumar plans to pen a book on SQL and Business Intelligence that can be easily comprehendible to newbies.

An avid reader of technical books, Sivakumar cherishes spending time with his family—especially playing with his 2-year-old son, Sachin.

My heartfelt thanks to the editorial and management team at Packt Publishing for again entrusting me with the wonderful opportunity of providing insightful review to this great title. I am grateful to the almighty God for enriching me with the knowledge and strength for this review. Last but not least, my sincere thanks to my caring parents; loving wife, Saranya; and my lovely son, Sachin for all their love, affection, and continuous support, and for always being there as a driving force.

www.PacktPub.com

Support files, eBooks, discount offers, and more

For support files and downloads related to your book, please visit www.PacktPub.com.

Did you know that Packt offers eBook versions of every book published, with PDF and ePub files available? You can upgrade to the eBook version at www.PacktPub.com and as a print book customer, you are entitled to a discount on the eBook copy. Get in touch with us at service@packtpub.com for more details.

At www.PacktPub.com, you can also read a collection of free technical articles, sign up for a range of free newsletters and receive exclusive discounts and offers on Packt books and eBooks.

https://www2.packtpub.com/books/subscription/packtlib

Do you need instant solutions to your IT questions? PacktLib is Packt's online digital book library. Here, you can search, access, and read Packt's entire library of books.

Why subscribe?
- Fully searchable across every book published by Packt
- Copy and paste, print, and bookmark content
- On demand and accessible via a web browser

Free access for Packt account holders

If you have an account with Packt at www.PacktPub.com, you can use this to access PacktLib today and view 9 entirely free books. Simply use your login credentials for immediate access.

Instant updates on new Packt books

Get notified! Find out when new books are published by following @PacktEnterprise on Twitter or the *Packt Enterprise* Facebook page.

Table of Contents

Preface

Data mining is a process of analyzing large and complex datasets to generate meaningful information from it. Today, we are living in the age of data explosion; the rate of digital data produced has grown exponentially over the years, which has opened new dimensions of data analysis like never before. With hardware and storage costs reducing drastically, enterprises can now afford to store huge volumes of data that was left uncaptured before. They can also derive a few insights from it. Data mining (sometimes called data or knowledge discovery) is the process of analyzing and visualizing data from different perspectives and summarizing it into useful information. This information can be used to increase revenue, cut costs, and perform predictive analysis to take more meaningful business decisions.

Data mining – what's the need?

Before understanding the need for data mining, it is important to understand the different forms of information extraction techniques available and the differences between them. The most commonly used terms are as follows:

- Information extraction
- Analysis
- Data mining

We will consider them one by one and try to dig deeper as to how different they are from data mining, or how different data mining is from each one of them.

Information extraction

This technique deals with extracting the structured information from documents that are either unstructured or are partly structured. The most common activity that closely relates to the extraction of information is the processing of the human texts using the techniques of Natural Language Processing (NLP). The most common implementation of information extraction can be seen in the field, where information is extracted from any media (audio, video, and so on) files.

Since the scope of information extraction is vast; currently, there is always an ongoing research on this topic, and the implementation of this technique is currently very restricted and fixed with a lot of rules to be followed. Based on this, a new report can be written as follows:

Tata Motors declared their acquisition of the Jaguar Land Rover

This can fit into an informational relation of Merger (company, company) and so on. Thus, IE allows us to perform some computation on the previously unstructured data and allows certain inferences to be drawn based on the logical reasoning and content of the data. It also allows us to provide a structure to the unstructured data.

Information extraction methodologies

There are always new approaches to information extraction that makes headlines every now and then. The Web is filled with tons of whitepapers discussing these approaches. A couple of such approaches are as follows:

- A statistics-based method (for example, the node information threshold algorithm)
- A template-based extraction (for example, the XQuery templates)

Data analysis

Data analysis is a process where you run some algorithms on your data to gain meaningful insight from it. This can help you determine trends, patterns, and take better decisions for your business. It is important to understand that data is of no use unless it is transformed to information through analysis. Data analysis uses a wide range of techniques, software, tools, and methods that:

- Will extract the data from an existing data store (the reason why data store is used here is because the source of data can be either a data warehouse or an OLTP database)

- Will discover abnormal trends by doing a trend analysis
- Will match the observed trends with the trends derived from the data to do a comparative analysis

The most common way of extracting the information from the data store is through a query. A query can be basic (for example, select Q4 sales from SalesProductInfo) or can comprise a series of joins. It might even pull data from multiple data sources and multiple applications (for example, Oracle and SQL Server).

The data that is extracted with the help of the queries is converted into a presentable manner with the help of a reporting tool. Usually, the reports might be in a tabular form or might be in a spreadsheet-formatted form with some graphics or drill down. Some reporting solutions might present the data in the bare form, while some other tools might provide some beautification to the data.

In today's world where data is gold, it becomes imperative to think of some of the methodologies of enforcing the security policies on the data in the sense that only some users can access a portion of data, while others cannot. Also, there are tools that provide the facility to design ad hoc reports.

Online analytical processing

A technology that's making waves in data analysis is Online Analytical Processing (OLAP). Data is organized into multidimensional hierarchies called cubes. Data mining algorithms assist in uncovering relationships or patterns based on some fixed algorithms.

OLAP tools allow you to slice and dice the data to extract the specific data items. For example, a cube that contains sales information is categorized by product, region, salesperson, retail outlet, and time period, in both units and dollars. Using an OLAP tool, a user needs to only click on a dimension to see a breakdown of dollar sales by region; an analysis of units by product, salesperson, and region; or to examine a particular salesperson's performance over a period of time.

There are various tools that are available on the market where the data can be presented in a graphical format, as visualization is very important in lending meaning to data. Some of the most famous tools are SQL Server Reporting Services; there are tools such as Power View and Power Query, which lends beautiful effects to the report and yields some very important insights to the data. Further discussion about the reporting services is covered in a later chapter; discussion about Power View is beyond the scope of this book.

Data mining

Data mining is the process by which we determine the patterns from a dataset with the help of some algorithms. The identification of patterns goes through several phases, such as data preparation, data modeling, data complexity considerations, visual interpretations of the data trends, and model updating process.

It is worthwhile to note that data mining is often interpreted as a system that will help us to take business decisions. While this is partially correct, this is not exactly the intended purpose of the data mining process.

Data mining is done based on some operations of the given data. The following topics summarize these operations that intertwine with data mining:

- Data cleansing
- Detect the relationship between the data
- Identify patterns from a set of data—data mining
- Detect automatic patterns once the algorithm is trained
- Use of the information and data for visual representation of the findings

Data mining can be summarized by saying that data mining processes historical data to find out the most appropriate action items in case similar situations arise, for example, if there is any product release happening, what should be my strategy to ensure that the sales are good.

Data mining can be used to predict the aftermath of a particular phenomenon (for example, what has been the trend of the global economy, and how can the growth in global economy lead to the migration of the population). Data mining can also be used to compete against other products and predict who (which organization) is more successful in luring the customers and why.

It is worthwhile to note that there are efforts being made to implement some standards for data mining. At present, there are standards defined for each aspect such as attributes of a data modeling activity. They are as follows:

- Process Standards: Cross Industry Standard Process for Data Mining (CRISP-DM)
- XML Standards: Common Warehouse Model for Data Mining (CWM-DM)
- Standard APIs: SQL/MM, Java API (JSR-73), and Microsoft OLE-DB

- Protocol for transport of remote and distributed data: Data Space Transport Protocol (DSTP)
- Model Scoring Standard: Predictive scoring and update protocol (PSUP)
- Web Standards: XML for analysis (XMLA)
- Grid Standards: Open Grid Service Architecture

Data mining for gaming

When we discuss data mining for gaming, the most prominent area where the data mining implementation is most prominent is in the extraction of patterns of user interaction from a tablebase.

A tablebase is a database that contains the analysis of a game based on the past interaction of the users. The following are the games where these strategies are most actively used:

- Chess
- Dots and Boxes
- Hex

The study and the application of the data mining techniques on the tablebase lend better prediction capability to the software. The following prominent personalities are involved in the pattern recognition of these games:

- Elwyn Berlekamp in Dot and Boxes
- John Nunn in Chess

Data mining for business

Data mining finds its use extensively in businesses where our ultimate objective is to determine the hidden trends that are not to be uncovered by other analytical means. For example, while performing market analysis to determine the customer base that should be targeted when a new product is launched, we can then launch several marketing campaigns to reach out to the selected customer base.

Human Resources use data mining to understand the factors that make their employees successful. Data mining can help us translate corporate goals into employee goals.

Not only decision making, but the data mining process has also helped us in learning from the past. For example, suppose we have been following a test procedure for a manufacturing industry, we use data mining to identify the problem areas that have been associated with a product and try to draw a parallel line with the testing process that has been used for the past release cycles in that organization. Thus, we can change our testing process for the upcoming product releases and expect to have fewer problems in that component.

Data mining techniques have been used in semiconductor manufacturing environments where we do not have enough past data with us, and there is a very complex and delicate relationship between several physical and chemical factors of the process.

The data mining process is also used to identify the past trends and instances that has affected the manufacturing process. It is also used to make the manufacturing process more effective and efficient and to reduce the breakdown and increase the production throughput.

Data mining for spatial data

The amount of geographical data that exists in our world today and the amount of data being added on an everyday basis is huge. The patterns and knowledge that it holds might give us enough foresight of the changes that we can expect on our planet's ecosystem.

Some of the areas where data mining plays a pivotal role along with the geographic information systems are as follows:

- Determine the impact of the land usage pattern on the climate
- Determine the usage of natural resources based on the population concentration

Data mining for sensor data

Sensors are everywhere nowadays, and an enormous amount of data is captured by sensors on a daily basis. In fact, sensors interact with human beings more often than we think, and the sensor data holds important information. Sensor data can be used to determine:

- Elements that a customer looks at when they pick up an item from a supermarket

- The number of average visitors to a particular place
- The most popular commodities in a particular place

Looking for correlation

There are many examples where we can see that any two occurrences are interrelated. These correlations might not be evident at first sight, but a closer look and application of the mining data from the warehouse will bring out the correlation and make it more apparent.

For example, if we were to ask ourselves the question as to what are the most common food items sold along with beer at any pub, or what are the most common items that any biker will carry when going on a long ride, will only help businesses to invest the money in the commodity that is more likely to be sold, and reap more return on investments. The correlation can be between any two activities; some of the areas where we can draw a correlation are as follows:

- Elections and poverty
- Wars and economy
- Economy and space adventures

This book is targeted towards SQL Server developers who want to be one step ahead in the data mining industry. The current era is all about predicting trends and recommending services, so this book will offer the reader an extra edge in the domain of data mining requirements.

What this book covers

Chapter 1, Identifying, Staging, and Understanding Data, will look at the first three stages of the data mining activity that comprises of identifying the need for data mining followed by staging and understanding the data.

Chapter 2, Data Model Preparation and Deployment, concentrates on the preparation of the data mining models and their deployment.

Chapter 3, Tools of the Trade, discusses SQL Server BI Suite that comprises of the SQL Server Integration Services, SQL Server Analysis Services, and SQL Server Reporting Services.

Chapter 4, Preparing the Data, concentrates on building the data warehouse database from diverse data sources followed by identification of the various facts and measures, and then developing a data mart for further reporting.

Chapter 5, Classification Models, provides an in-depth look into the various classification models provided by the SQL Server Data Mining platform.

Chapter 6, Segmentation and Association Models, provides an in-depth look into the various segmentation and association algorithms provided by the SQL Server Data Mining platform.

Chapter 7, Sequence and Regression Models, provides an in-depth look into the various sequencing and regression algorithms provided by the SQL Server Data Mining platform.

Chapter 8, Data Mining Using Excel and Big Data, teaches you how to mine through the data with the help of the Excel add-in and also uses Microsoft's Big Data Offering (HDInsight) to perform data mining and analysis of data.

Chapter 9, Tuning the Models, covers the aspects that will help us design models for optimum performance. We will look at the factors that should be considered for attribute-based data mining, prediction-based data mining, and clustering-based data mining.

Chapter 10, Troubleshooting, covers a few troubleshooting tips and techniques to debug algorithms, Business Intelligence solutions, and also various logs that we can use.

What you need for this book

You will need the following software:

- SQL Server 2014 CTP2
- AdvenutureWorks OLTP Database for 2012 (compatible with 2014)
- AdventureWorksDW Database for 2012 (compatible with 2014)

Who this book is for

This book is for readers who are already familiar with Microsoft SQL Server and relational database management system concepts and technologies. If you are looking forward to learning SQL Server 2014 from scratch, this book is not for you. A basic understanding of Business Intelligence and data analysis/mining concepts will be a very helpful prerequisite.

Conventions

In this book, you will find a number of styles of text that distinguish between different kinds of information. Here are some examples of these styles, and an explanation of their meaning.

Code words in text, database table names, folder names, filenames, file extensions, pathnames, dummy URLs, user input, and Twitter handles are shown as follows: "The MAXIMUM_STATES parameter imposes a limit on the number of discrete values or states that an attribute can have."

A block of code is set as follows:

```
SELECT FLATTENED MODEL_NAME,
(SELECT ATTRIBUTE_NAME, ATTRIBUTE_VALUE, [SUPPORT], [PROBABILITY],
VALUETYPE FROM NODE_DISTRIBUTION) AS t
FROM [v Target Mail].CONTENT
WHERE NODE_TYPE = 26;
```

Any command-line input or output is written as follows:

```
Hadoop fs -cp /user/<username>/nsl-forest /mahout
```

New terms and **important words** are shown in bold. Words that you see on the screen, in menus or dialog boxes for example, appear in the text like this: "We now switch to the **Query** mode."

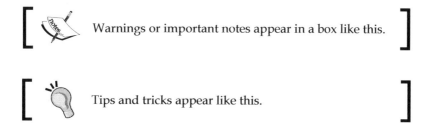

Warnings or important notes appear in a box like this.

Tips and tricks appear like this.

Reader feedback

Feedback from our readers is always welcome. Let us know what you think about this book—what you liked or may have disliked. Reader feedback is important for us to develop titles that you really get the most out of.

To send us general feedback, simply send an e-mail to feedback@packtpub.com, and mention the book title via the subject of your message.

If there is a topic that you have expertise in and you are interested in either writing or contributing to a book, see our author guide on www.packtpub.com/authors.

Customer support

Now that you are the proud owner of a Packt book, we have a number of things to help you to get the most from your purchase.

Downloading the example code

You can download the example code files for all Packt books you have purchased from your account at http://www.packtpub.com. If you purchased this book elsewhere, you can visit http://www.packtpub.com/support and register to have the files e-mailed directly to you.

Downloading the color images of this book

We also provide you with a PDF file that has color images of the screenshots/ diagrams used in this book. The color images will help you better understand the changes in the output. You can download this file from: https://www.packtpub. com/sites/default/files/downloads/8949EN_ColoredImages.pdf

Errata

Although we have taken every care to ensure the accuracy of our content, mistakes do happen. If you find a mistake in one of our books—maybe a mistake in the text or the code—we would be grateful if you would report this to us. By doing so, you can save other readers from frustration and help us improve subsequent versions of this book. If you find any errata, please report them by visiting http://www.packtpub. com/submit-errata, selecting your book, clicking on the **Errata Submission Form** link, and entering the details of your errata. Once your errata are verified, your submission will be accepted and the errata will be uploaded to our website or added to any list of existing errata under the Errata section of that title.

To view the previously submitted errata, go to https://www.packtpub.com/books/content/support and enter the name of the book in the search field. The required information will appear under the **Errata** section.

Piracy

Piracy of copyright material on the Internet is an ongoing problem across all media. At Packt, we take the protection of our copyright and licenses very seriously. If you come across any illegal copies of our works, in any form, on the Internet, please provide us with the location address or website name immediately so that we can pursue a remedy.

Please contact us at copyright@packtpub.com with a link to the suspected pirated material.

We appreciate your help in protecting our authors, and our ability to bring you valuable content.

Questions

You can contact us at questions@packtpub.com if you are having a problem with any aspect of the book, and we will do our best to address it.

1
Identifying, Staging, and Understanding Data

We will begin our discussion with an introduction to the data mining life cycle, and this chapter will focus on its first three stages. You are expected to have a basic understanding of the Microsoft Business Intelligence stack and familiarity of terms such as **extract, transform, and load** (ETL), data warehouse, and so on. This chapter builds on this basic understanding.

We will cover the following topics in this chapter:

- Data mining life cycle
- Identifying the goal
- Staging data
- Understanding and cleansing data

Data mining life cycle

Before going into further detail, it is important to understand the various stages of the data mining life cycle. The data mining life cycle can be broadly classified into the following steps:

1. Understanding the business requirement.
2. Understanding the data.
3. Preparing the data for analysis.
4. Preparing the data mining models.
5. Evaluating the results of the analysis prepared with the models.
6. Deploying the models to the SQL Server Analysis Services.
7. Repeating steps 1 to 6 in case the business requirement changes.

Let's look at each of these stages in detail.

First and foremost, the task that needs to be well defined even before beginning the mining process is to identify the goals. This is a crucial part of the data mining exercise and you need to understand the following questions:

- What and whom are we targeting?
- What is the outcome we are targeting?
- What is the time frame for which we have the data and what is the target time period that our data is going to forecast?
- What would the success measures look like?

Let's define a classic problem and understand more about the preceding questions. Note that for the most part of this book, we will be using the AdventureWorks and AdventureWorksDW databases for our data mining activities as they already have the schema and dimensions predefined. We can use them to discuss how to extract the information rather than spending our time on defining the schema.

The details on how to acquire the AdventureWorks database is already discussed in the Preface of this book.

Consider an instance where you are a salesman for the AdventureWorks Cycles, company, and you need to make predictions that could be used in marketing the products. The problem sounds simple and straightforward, but any serious data miner would immediately come up with many questions. Why? The answer lies in the exactness of the information being searched for. Let's discuss this in detail.

The problem statement comprises the words predictions and marketing. When we talk about predictions, there are several insights that we seek, namely:

- What is it that we are predicting? (for example: customers, product sales, and so on)
- What is the time period of the data that we are selecting for prediction?
- What time period are we going to have the prediction for?
- What is the expected outcome of the prediction exercise?

From the marketing point of view, several follow-up questions that must be answered are as follows:

- What is our target for marketing; a new product or an older product?
- Is our marketing strategy product centric or customer centric? Are we going to market our product irrespective of the customer classification, or are we marketing our product according to customer classification?
- On what timeline in the past is our marketing going to be based on?

We might observe that there are many questions that overlap the two categories and, therefore, there is an opportunity to consolidate the questions and classify them as follows:

- What is the population that we are targeting?
- What are the factors that we will actually be looking at?
- What is the time period of the past data that we will be looking at?
- What is the time period in the future that we will be considering the data mining results for?

Let's throw some light on these aspects based on the AdventureWorks example. We will get answers to the preceding questions and arrive at a more refined problem statement.

What is the population that we are targeting? The target population might be classified according to the following aspects:

- Age
- Salary
- Number of kids

What are the factors that we are actually looking at? They might be classified as follows:

- **Geographical location**: The people living in hilly areas would prefer **All Terrain Bikes (ATB)** and the population on plains would prefer daily commute bikes.
- **Household**: The people living in posh areas would look for bikes with the latest gears and also look for accessories that are state of the art, whereas people in the suburban areas would mostly look for budgetary bikes.
- **Affinity of components**: The people who tend to buy bikes would also buy some accessories.

What is the time period of the past data that we would be looking at? Usually, the data that we get is quite huge and often consists of the information that we might very adequately label as noise. In order to sieve effective information, we will have to determine exactly how much into the past we should look at; for example, we can look at the data for the past year, past two years, or past five years.

We also need to decide the future data that we will consider the data mining results for. We might be looking at predicting our market strategy for an upcoming festive season or throughout the year. We need to be aware that market trends change and so do people's needs and requirements. So we need to keep a time frame to refresh our findings to an optimal; for example, the predictions from the past five years' data can be valid for the upcoming two or three years depending upon the results that we get.

Now that we have taken a closer look into the problem, let's redefine the problem more accurately. AdventureWorks Cycles has several stores in various locations and, based on the location, we would like to get an insight into the following:

- Which products should be stocked where?
- Which products should be stocked together?
- How many products should be stocked?
- What is the trend of sales for a new product in an area?

It is not necessary that we receive answers to all the detailed questions but even if we keep looking for the answers to these questions, there would be several insights that we will get, which will help us make better business decisions.

Staging data

In this phase, we collect data from all the sources and dump them into a common repository, which can be any database system such as SQL Server, Oracle, and so on. Usually, an organization might have various applications to keep track of the data from various departments, and it is quite possible that all these applications might use a different database system to store the data. Thus, the staging phase is characterized by dumping the data from all the other data storage systems into a centralized repository.

Extract, transform, and load

This term is most common when we talk about data warehouse. As it is clear, ETL has the following three parts:

- **Extract**: The data is extracted from a different source database and other databases that might contain the information that we seek
- **Transform**: Some transformation is applied to the data to fit the operational needs, such as cleaning, calculation, removing duplicates, reformatting, and so on
- **Load**: The transformed data is loaded into the destination data store database

We usually believe that the ETL is only required till we load the data onto the data warehouse but this is not true. ETL can be used anywhere that we feel the need to do some transformation of data as shown in the following figure:

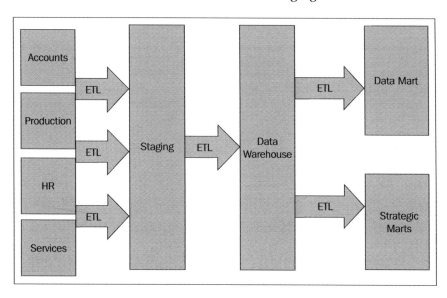

Data warehouse

As evident from the preceding figure, the next stage is the data warehouse. The AdventureWorksDW database is the outcome of the ETL applied to the staging database, which is AdventureWorks. We will now discuss the concepts of data warehousing and some best practices, and then relate to these concepts with the help of the AdventureWorksDW database.

Measures and dimensions

There are a few common terminologies you will encounter as you enter the world of data warehousing. This section discusses them to help you get familiar:

- **Measure**: Any business entity that can be aggregated or whose values can be ascertained in a numerical value is termed as measure, for example, sales, number of products, and so on

- **Dimension**: This is any business entity that lends some meaning to the measures, for example, in an organization, the quantity of goods sold is a measure but the month is a dimension

Schema

Basically, a schema determines the relationship of the various entities with each other. There are essentially two types of schema, namely:

- **Star schema**: This is a relationship where the measures have a direct relationship with the dimensions. Let's look at an instance wherein a seller has several stores that sell several products. The relationship of the tables based on the star schema will be as shown in the following screenshot:

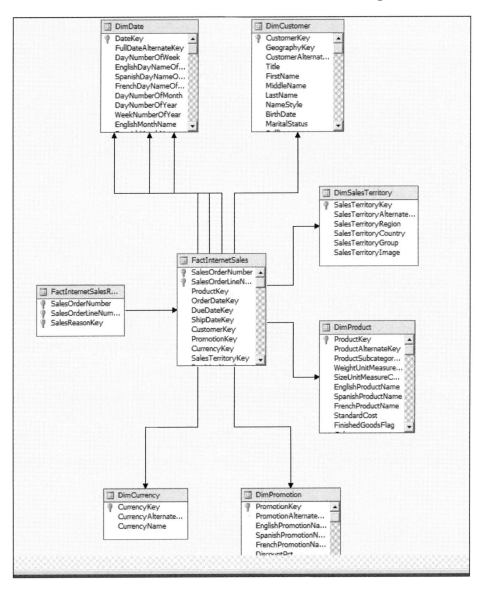

- **Snowflake schema**: This is a relationship wherein the measures may have a direct and indirect relationship with the dimensions. We will be designing a snowflake schema if we want a more detailed drill down of the data. Snowflake schema would usually involve hierarchies, as shown in the following screenshot:

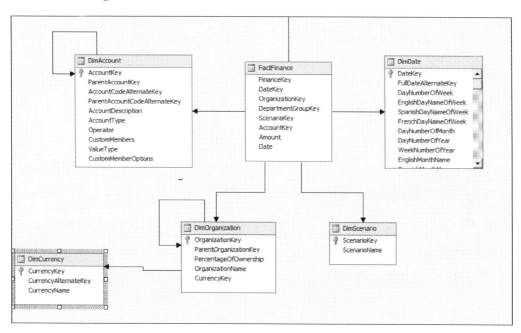

Data mart

While a data warehouse is a more organization-wide repository of data, extracting data from such a huge repository might well be an uphill task. We segregate the data according to the department or the specialty that the data belongs to, so that we have much smaller sections of the data to work with and extract information from. We call these smaller data warehouses data marts.

Let's consider the sales for AdventureWorks Cycles. To make any predictions on the sales of AdventureWorks Cycles, we will have to group all the tables associated with the sales together in a data mart. Based on the AdventureWorks database, we have the following table in the AdventureWorks sales data mart.

The Internet sales facts table has the following data:

```
[ProductKey]
 [OrderDateKey]
```

```
[DueDateKey]
[ShipDateKey]
[CustomerKey]
[PromotionKey]
[CurrencyKey]
[SalesTerritoryKey]
[SalesOrderNumber]
[SalesOrderLineNumber]
[RevisionNumber]
[OrderQuantity]
[UnitPrice]
[ExtendedAmount]
[UnitPriceDiscountPct]
[DiscountAmount]
[ProductStandardCost]
[TotalProductCost]
[SalesAmount]
[TaxAmt]
[Freight]
[CarrierTrackingNumber]
[CustomerPONumber]
[OrderDate]
[DueDate]
[ShipDate]
```

From the preceding column, we can easily identify that if we need to separate the tables to perform the sales analysis alone, we can safely include the following:

- **Product**: This provides the following data:
  ```
  [ProductKey]
  [ListPrice]
  ```

- **Date**: This provides the following data:
  ```
  [DateKey]
  ```

- **Customer**: This provides the following data:
  ```
  [CustomerKey]
  ```

- **Currency**: This provides the following data:
  ```
  [CurrencyKey]
  ```

- **Sales territory**: This provides the following data:
  ```
  [SalesTerritoryKey]
  ```

The preceding data will provide the relevant dimensions and the facts that are already contained in the FactInternetSales table and, hence, we can easily perform all the analysis pertaining to the sales of the organization.

Refreshing data

Based on the nature of the business and the requirements of the analysis, refreshing of data can be done either in parts wherein new or incremental data is added to the tables, or we can refresh the entire data wherein the tables are cleaned and filled with new data, which consists of the old and new data.

Let's discuss the preceding points in the context of the AdventureWorks database. We will take the employee table to begin with. The following is the list of columns in the employee table:

```
[BusinessEntityID]
, [NationalIDNumber]
, [LoginID]
, [OrganizationNode]
, [OrganizationLevel]
, [JobTitle]
, [BirthDate]
, [MaritalStatus]
, [Gender]
, [HireDate]
, [SalariedFlag]
, [VacationHours]
, [SickLeaveHours]
, [CurrentFlag]
, [rowguid]
, [ModifiedDate]
```

Considering an organization in the real world, we do not have a large number of employees leaving and joining the organization. So, it will not really make sense to have a procedure in place to reload the dimensions. Prior to SQL 2008. We have to follow the method described in the next section to keep track of the changes. SQL 2008 provides us with **Change Data Capture** (**CDC**) and **Change Tracking** (**CT**), which will help us in incremental loading of our data warehouse; however, the following solution presented is a generalized solution that will work for any source database. When it comes to managing the changes in the dimensions table, **Slowly Changing Dimensions** (**SCD**) is worth a mention. We will briefly look at the SCD here. There are three types of SCD, namely:

- **Type 1**: The older values are overwritten by new values
- **Type 2**: A new row specifying the present value for the dimension is inserted
- **Type 3**: The column specifying `TimeStamp` from which the new value is effective is updated

Let's take the example of `HireDate` as a method of keeping track of the incremental loading. We will also have to maintain a small table that will keep a track of the data that is loaded from the `employee` table. So, we create a table as follows:

```
Create table employee_load_status(
HireDate    DateTime,
LoadStatus          varchar
);
```

The following script will load the `employee` table from the AdventureWorks database to the `DimEmployee` table in the AdventureWorksDW database:

```
With employee_loaded_date(HireDate)   as
(select   ISNULL(Max(HireDate),to_date('01-01-1900','MM-DD-YYYY')) from
employee_load_status where LoadStatus='success'
Union All
Select ISNULL(min(HireDate),to_date('01-01-1900','MM-DD-YYYY'))  from
employee_load_status where LoadStatus='failed'
)
Insert into DimEmployee  select * from employee where HireDate
>=(select Min(HireDate) from employee_loaded_date);
```

This will reload all the data from the date of the first failure till the present day.

A similar procedure can be followed to load the fact table but there is a catch. If we look at the sales table in the AdventureWorks database, we see the following columns:

```
[BusinessEntityID]
, [TerritoryID]
, [SalesQuota]
, [Bonus]
, [CommissionPct]
, [SalesYTD]
, [SalesLastYear]
, [rowguid]
, [ModifiedDate]
```

The `SalesYTD` column might change with every passing day, so do we perform a full load every day or do we perform an incremental load based on date? This will depend upon the procedure used to load the data in the sales table and the `ModifiedDate` column.

Assuming the `ModifiedDate` column reflects the date on which the load was performed, we also see that there is no table in the AdventureWorksDW that will use the `SalesYTD` field directly. We will have to apply some transformation to get the values of `OrderQuantity`, `DateOfShipment`, and so on.

Let's look at this with a simpler example. Consider we have the following sales table:

Name	SalesAmount	Date
Rama	1000	11-02-2014
Shyama	2000	11-02-2014

Consider we have the following fact table:

id	SalesAmount	Datekey

We will have to think of whether to apply incremental load or a complete reload of the table based on our end needs. So the entries for the incremental load will look like this:

id	SalesAmount	Datekey
ra	1000	11-02-2014
Sh	2000	11-02-2014
Ra	4000	12-02-2014
Sh	5000	13-02-2014

Also, a complete reload will appear as shown here:

id	TotalSalesAmount	Datekey
Ra	5000	12-02-2014
Sh	7000	13-02-2014

Notice how the `SalesAmount` column changes to `TotalSalesAmount` depending on the load criteria.

Understanding and cleansing data

Before entering the warehouse, the data should go through several cleaning operations. These involve shaping up the raw data through transformation, null value removals, duplicate removals, and so on. In this section, we will discuss the techniques and methodologies pertaining to the understanding and cleansing of the data, we will see how we can identify the data that we need to cleanse, and how we will set a benchmark for the data sanity for further data refresh.

Data cleansing is the act of detecting the data that is either out of sync, not accurate, or incomplete, and we either correct, delete, or synchronize the data so that the chances of any ambiguity or inaccuracy in any prediction that is based on this data is minimized.

When we talk about data cleansing, we definitely need to have a basic data benchmark in place—a dataset against which the incoming data can be compared. Or, there needs to be a set of conditions or criteria against which the incoming data needs to be compared. Once the data is compared and we have a list of deviation of the data from the criteria for data sanity, we can very easily correct the deviation or delete the data with the deviation.

We will now get more specific on the meaning of the benchmark data or the set of conditions. The following are some of the situations that would help us to get a deeper understanding of what criteria a benchmark data will possess:

- The data will have a very high conformance to the constraints or rules of the data store such as the target data type, the target data ranges, the target foreign key constraints, the target unique constraints, and so on.

- The data should not be incomplete, for example, some of the data or group of data should together add up to a fixed total. We need to make sure that such a total exists in the data store.

- The data should be consistent. We might get the data feed from various sources but the data needs to be in the common format, the most common example is `customerid`. The accounts department might have `customerid` as `C<number>` but the sales department might have the same details as `ID<number>`. In such cases, it is very important to understand how the data is stored in different databases and how can we apply different data transformations so that the data is finally loaded in the main database or in the warehouse in a consistent manner.

  In continuation with the preceding point, there might be a situation wherein the data might be pooled in from different regions in which case, we might experience a difference in the locales that would give rise to complications, such as differences in the currency, differences in the units of measurement of weights, and so on. In such a situation, the task of combining the data is even more difficult and requires more stages of transformation.

Thus, as we see from the preceding discussion, a benchmark data would have the following aspects:

- Higher conformance to the constraints
- Higher degree of completeness
- Higher consistency
- Lower locale-specific variations

The preceding task of ensuring high quality data might seem to be an uphill task and might not be feasible for a human being; therefore, we have many tools that are at our disposal, which possess the ability to analyze the incoming data, detect any variation from the defined standard, suggest the correction, and even correct the data for us if we so desire. One such tool that we will be using in our scenario is the **Data Quality Services (DQS)**.

DQS is a knowledge-based product that is available with the SQL Server and can be installed as a part of the SQL Server installation.

Rather than going into the discussion of the DQS, we will go through a practical example here and see how the DQS makes our task of maintaining the data quality easier and also ensures a high degree of data quality.

The first thing that we need to do to have a data quality project is to create a knowledge base. We will have to start an instance of **Data Quality Client**.

Once started, the screen will look this:

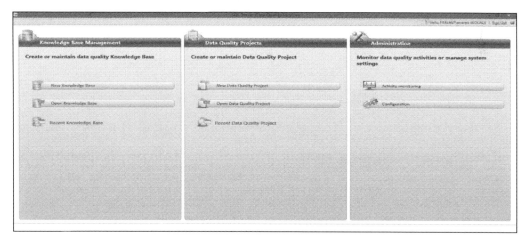

Start-up screen of the Data Quality Client

We will now create a new knowledge base by clicking on the **New Knowledge Base** button, as shown in the following screenshot:

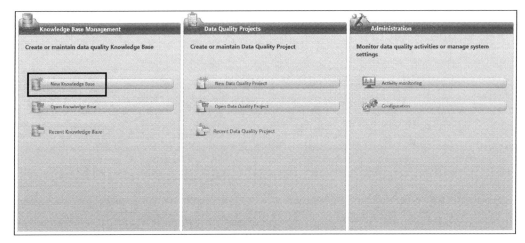

Data Quality Client screen

This opens up the new **Knowledge Base Management** window, as shown here:

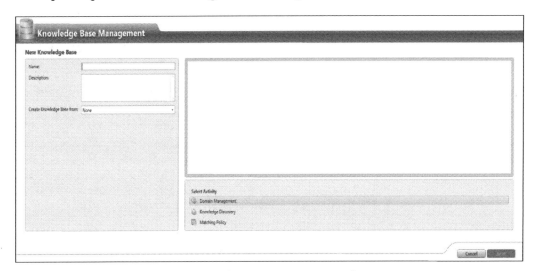

The Knowledge Base Management interface

Now, we will have to decide which columns we are going to have as our reference. In AdventureWorksDW, we take CustomerAlternateKey, MaritalStatus, and Gender from the table DimCustomer as KnowledgeBase.

We will now develop knowledge base as follows:

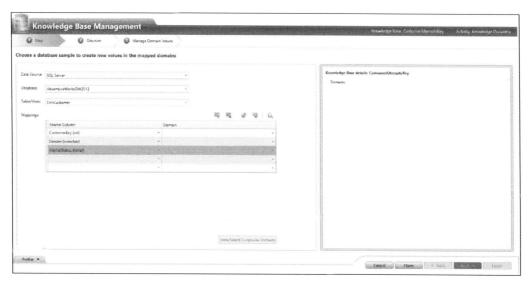

Selecting the source of the data

Click on the icon, as shown in the following screenshot, to create a domain. We will create a unique domain for every column:

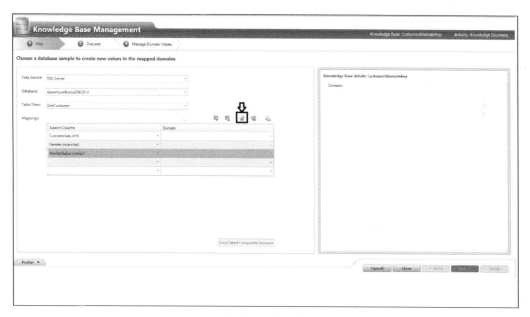

Creating a Domain

Click on the **Next** button to start the data discovery and we will reach the following screen:

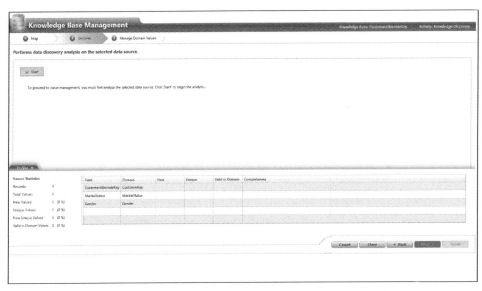

Starting the Data Discovery Process once the Domains for the Fields have been created

In the following screenshot, we can see that **CustomerAlternateKey** has all the unique values, the **MaritalStatus** column has **2** unique values and the **Gender** column has **2** unique values:

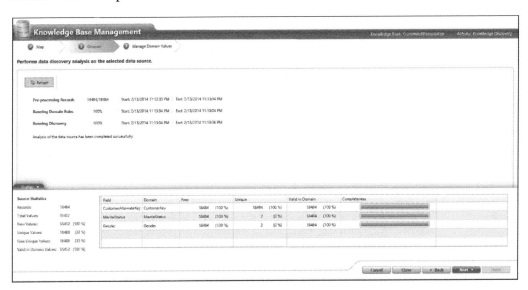

Unique values contained in each column

Then, we reach the following screen that gives us detailed data for each column:

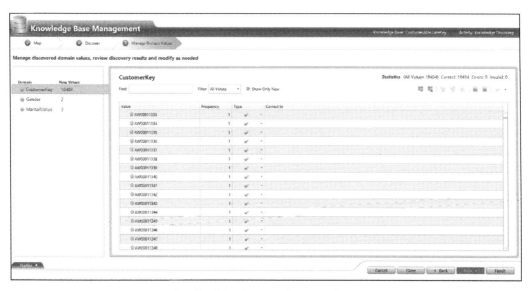

Results of the discovery for each column

When we click on the **Finish** button, we will see the following screen:

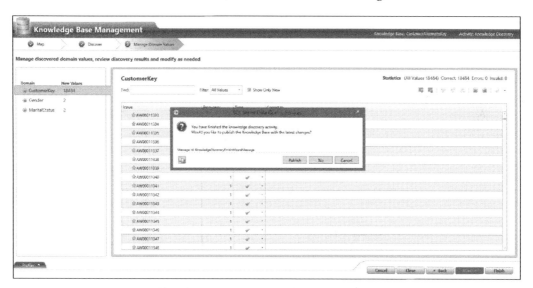

We publish this knowledge base to be used for other datasets

We will now click on **Publish** and we have a base data ready to test the sanity of other datasets.

Let's induce some anomaly in the data by changing the first record of the
`DimCustomer` table as follows:

Columnname	PreviousValue	NextValue	ChangedValue
CustomerAlternateKey	AW00011002		00011002
MaritalStatus	M	N	
Gender	M	N	

Now, let's apply the DQS implementation over this new table and see the results. We
can click on **New Data Quality Project**, as shown here:

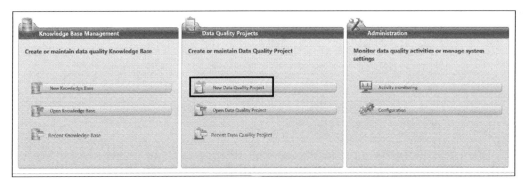

Starting a New Data Quality Project

We name the project as `testSanity`, and select the activity as **Cleaning**, as shown in
the following screenshot:

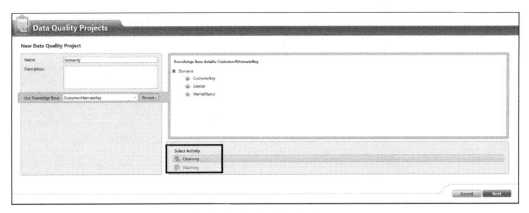

Project is for cleaning the data

We now click on **Next** and reach the next screen where we need to select the table to be cleansed, as shown here:

The Map tab in Data Quality Project

The remaining fields will be populated automatically. We now click on **Next** and start the analysis to arrive at the following screenshot:

The CustomerKey details in Data Quality Project

We now highlight the **Gender** domain to see the suggestion and the confidence for this suggestion, as shown here:

The Gender details in Data Quality Project

The confidence and suggestion for **MaritalStatus** is as shown in the following screenshot:

The MartialStatus details in Data Quality Project

The **Confidence** column is the certainty with which the DQS is suggesting the changes in the value. So, we can see that it suggests the change in **CustomerAlternateKey** with a confidence of 73 percent, but it suggests the addition of the values of **MaritalStatus** and **Gender** as **N** with a confidence of 0 percent, which we can approve or ignore.

Summary

In this chapter, we've covered the first three steps of any data mining process. We've considered the reasons why we would want to undertake a data mining activity and identified the goal we have in mind. We then looked to stage the data and cleanse it. In the next chapter, we will look at how the SQL Server Business Intelligence Suite will help us work with this data.

2

Data Model Preparation and Deployment

In the previous chapter, we covered the first three phases of the data mining life cycle, namely, identifying, staging, and understanding data; this chapter will cover the remaining three phases of data mining, which are as follows:

- Preparing data models
- Validating data models
- Deploying data models

Preparing data models

This section will outline the business problem that we intend to solve and help you decide on the algorithm that would be used to get us the required predictions. We will discuss the data mining algorithms available from the Microsoft suite and their usage.

Cross-Industry Standard Process for Data Mining

The discussion of data mining standards is important because it forms the basic framework for the data mining process in many organizations. The survey conducted by KDnuggets at `http://www.kdnuggets.com/polls/2007/data_mining_methodology.htm` clearly shows **Cross-Industry Standard Process for Data Mining (CRISP-DM)** as the winner.

The following diagram shows an outline of the CRISP-DM methodology:

The first stage, as shown in the preceding figure, is the **Business Understanding** phase, which has the prime objective of understanding the end objective from a business perspective. How will these results transform into business results? This phase is one of the important phases as it would help us to put the data mining effort in the right direction and get the results that would help us take proper business decisions.

The **Data Understanding** phase is the phase where we collect data from different sources, try to understand the relationship between different key attributes, and understand whether the data representation is uniform or requires some transformations.

The **Data Preparation** phase involves segregating the unwanted data from the data on which we are going to do our analysis. This phase will also involve activities such as cleaning of the data, calculation of some additional attributes, merging the data from two databases, and tables to form a single uniform record or aggregation.

The **Modeling** phase is characterized by the selection of the modeling tool and preliminary assessment of the data mining models. The parameter settings for the various models and the assessment of the models according to the success criteria will be the activities in this phase.

While the test in the **Modeling** phase dealt with accuracy of the models, the **Evaluation** phase is where the actual accuracy measurement, in terms of meeting the business objectives, is done. This is the phase where we will also figure out whether there is a reason to go in for remodeling.

The **Deployment** phase will be where we will document our maintenance and monitoring strategy for models. A proper implementation of this phase will avoid usage of wrong predictions, or less accurate predictions, and will also ensure that the models are up to date with the changing data.

As evident in the preceding diagram, we can go back and forth between various stages in the CRISP-DM model; this is important because it is not always possible to have crystal clear objectives before we proceed with data mining. We might not even know the business and therefore not be in a position to decide what our objectives should be. But as we proceed with the various stages, we will have a better understanding of the business and hence be able to form an effective problem statement.

We will discuss the business problem before we think about modeling, as having a clear understanding of the business problem will aid us in choosing the most effective algorithm for the solution of the business problem. We will come back to this diagram in the subsequent topics.

The following diagram provides a brief overview of the hierarchy in the data mining solution:

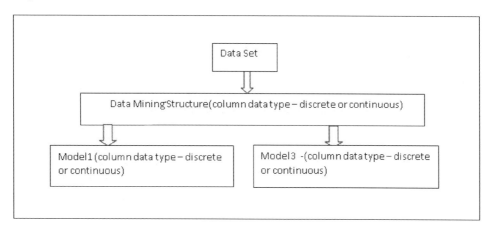

As we can see from the preceding diagram, a data mining structure contains many data mining models and the data type for the columns are defined at the structure level and the model level. We will discuss the types of variables here. There are several types of variables, but we will only discuss the most commonly used ones in the following section.

The discrete variable has only specific values and there are no continuous values; gender of an individual is one example of the discrete variable.

The continuous variable has values that cannot be categorized into any particular bucket and therefore they will have a range of values. The quarter-on-quarter sales of the organization is an example of the continuous variable.

In certain scenarios, we might have to discretize a continuous content type either because the algorithm that we are using only supports the discrete content type or our business models wants discrete content types. In these circumstances, the value of the variable is categorized into several buckets so that these groups can be used by the algorithms. An example of this can be the sales for the years ranging from 1991 to 2014; this data has to be divided into several buckets depending upon the algorithm used. There are several ways in which the data can be categorized into several buckets. If we allow the Analysis Services to perform the discretization, the formula used will be: *Number of buckets = sqrt(n)* where *n* is the number of distinct values for a column.

The key content types are used for columns when that column is going to be used to uniquely identify the record rather than use the column for analysis.

A column also has the associated attributes that might reside in the same table or in a different table, for example, the product identified by the ProductID key might have the attributes such as `productname`, `productbatch`, and the sales in number of units.

A column for a model can serve as an input column, output column or both. If we do not want a column to be used in the analysis, we can set the usage property of that column to ignore.

The data is divided into testing and training sets at the structure level; by default, 70 percent of the data is used to train the model, while 30 percent of the data is used to test the model. The data could also be divided based on a number of cases. A case represents a state of data in which attributes have specific values. If we limit the number of cases to 1000, there will be 1000 such arrangements of different attributes against which the model would be trained.

As we go along training and testing our models, these concepts will be highlighted wherever used.

Let's now have a brief discussion about the various data mining algorithms available in the Microsoft suite.

The following are the major classifications of the data mining algorithms:

- **Classification algorithms**: These algorithms preliminarily help in determining the values of the discrete values in a dataset based on other attributes in the dataset. The classification algorithms that are available in Analysis Services are Decision Trees, Naïve Bayes, Clustering, and Neural Network.

- **Regression algorithms**: These algorithms preliminarily help in determining the values of continuous variables in a dataset based on other attributes in the dataset. The regression algorithms that are available in Analysis Services are Time Series, Linear Regression, and Decision Trees.

- **Segmentation algorithms**: These help in understanding the relationship between different attributes by classifying them based on similarity of properties. The segmentation algorithm that is available in Analysis Services is the clustering algorithm.

- **Association algorithms**: The most common usage of these algorithms is to determine the relationship between different attributes in a dataset. The association algorithm that is available in Analysis Services is Association and Decision Trees.

- **Sequence analysis algorithms**: These algorithms are used to analyze the sequence path or flow of user interaction with a particular system. In terms of data, these determine the hierarchical relationship between different datasets. The sequence algorithm that is available in Analysis Services is Sequence Clustering.

Now let's decide upon a business requirement and then decide which algorithm we will be using. The following are some of the various scenarios that we will look at (we can also correlate them to our real life):

- AdventureWorks Cycles wants to understand whether a particular customer will ever return to buy products, given the past record of the customer such as age and geographical location.

- AdventureWorks Cycles wants to understand the customers in order to plan its marketing campaign, which is sending out the fliers based on the past data of the customers who responded to the e-mail.

- AdventureWorks Cycles wants to predict the sales of the cycle models based on the past year's sales and understand whether or not a particular model should be continued.

- Nowadays, there are more customers that have their presence online than those who prefer to walk into stores physically to do some shopping; therefore, we need to understand the sequences of the web page visits of the customers too. We also need to understand the links that a customer would most likely click on. The positioning of the links on the website and the data points will serve as an input to restructure the website, so that the links and the advertisements are positioned accordingly to get maximum output in terms of clicks.

- Even if a customer walks into a store, there are some items that might have some affinity with each other, for example, if a customer walks into a store to buy a bicycle, he can also buy tire tubes, helmets, and knee pads and there are more chances of him buying the tire accessories than that of tire tubes. So, if we place the accessories section closer to the main product, it would be a good overall buying experience for the customer and vice versa. Thus, we need to understand what commodities should be placed closer to and together.

If we look at the first two scenarios, we are mostly looking for the values of some discrete variables with the answers as yes/no, such as will the customer buy another product or not. So, given our description of the classification algorithms, we can apply the techniques of the classification algorithms to the first two business problems.

For the third scenario, we are determining the values of the variable that has some continuity, for example, the sales of a commodity based on past sales. This is a continuous variable and therefore would fit into the description of regression algorithms.

For the fourth scenario, if we look more closely, we are looking at the sequence of the web link visits of the customer and hence we would be employing the sequence clustering algorithms here.

For the fifth scenario, we are looking at grouping the commodities, and therefore we might employ the clustering algorithm here.

Let's say that we are looking at the problem statement, AdventureWorks Cycles wants to restructure its company strategy and wants to consolidate its manufacturing process and improve its sales and marketing strategies. The company has sufficient data from the past and wants to use this data to gather information to determine:

- Which models should continue and/or discontinue

- How it should restructure its showroom

- How it should revamp its website

- Whether it needs a data mining exercise to be performed on its data

As the preceding business objective involves many different aspects of business, we will need to use many different algorithms. This also brings to light one very important fact that a data mining activity might involve more than one data mining model.

Since this scenario deals with receiving a yes/no type of answer along with the market basket analysis and the website flow, we will have to deploy the classification and the sequence clustering algorithms to solve the problem. Hence, we use the Microsoft Decision Tree Algorithm and Microsoft Sequence Clustering Algorithm to receive the prediction.

SQL Server provides a tool wherein we can design all the Business Intelligence solutions, which include the SQL Server Analysis Services multidimensional project, the reporting services project, and the integration services project, and then deploy them. This tool was called Business Intelligence Development Studio previously but is now known as the SQL Server Data Tools. We will be using the SQL Server Data Tools throughout this book and will often refer to it as SSDT.

Let's jump right into the implementation of a practical solution that will use each of the concepts described in this chapter.

Open the SQL Server Data Tools and select the **Analysis Services Multidimensional and Data Mining Project** type. At present, data mining is not supported by the tabular model data and therefore we will be using the multidimensional project for our example, shown in the following screenshot:

We now fill the following details:

- **Name:** TestDataMining
- **Location:** D:\DataMining\TestDataMining (you can choose a drive of your choice)
- **Solution name:** TestDataMining

Then, select the checkbox for **Create directory for solution** and click on **OK**. We now add a data source to the project by clicking on **Data Source** and then clicking on **New**, as shown here:

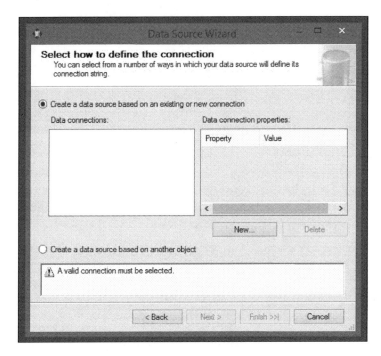

The list of available providers that the data source supports is shown here:

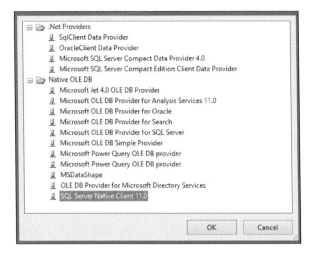

We click on **New** and then make the selection, as shown:

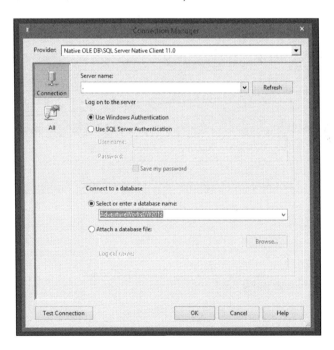

In the next screen, we select the **Use the service account** option and name the data source in the next screen as `TestDataMining` and then click on **Finish**.

We will now select the table perspective buyer and all the views for our data source. We can create new views as required, but at present the views present in the database will give us the information that we are looking for, as shown here:

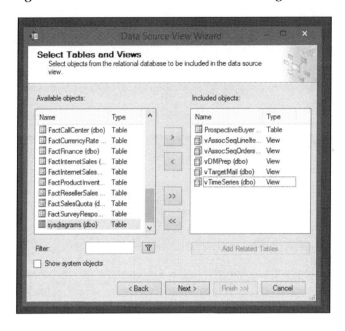

Click on **Next** and then on **Finish** to see the following screen:

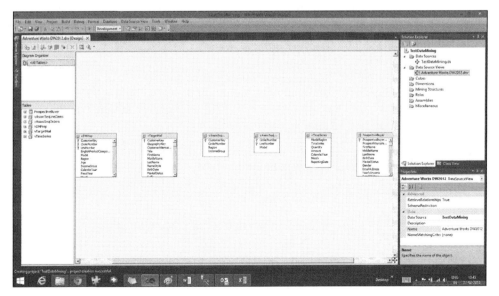

Data Source view showing the tables that were selected

Now that we have the data source ready, we will be moving on to use the data mining models and then validate them.

Validating data models

In this section, we will be preparing the data mining models and validating them. This section will be a continuation of the last section where we finished creating the data source views for our mining structure.

Preparing the data mining models

Right-click on **Mining Structures** and then click on **New**. We will be presented with the following screen:

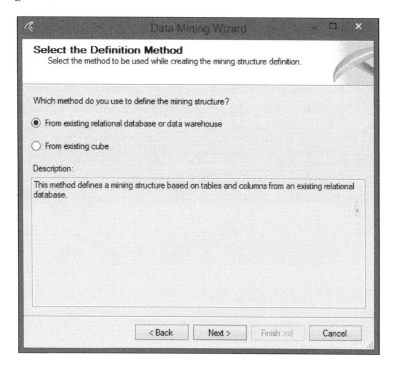

We now select the **Microsoft Decision Trees** algorithm, as shown here:

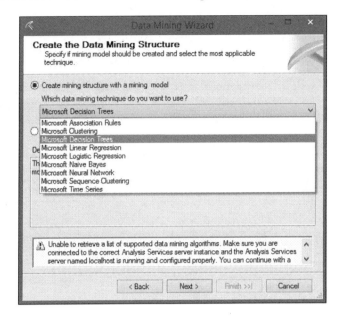

Then, we click on **Next** twice and reach the following screen:

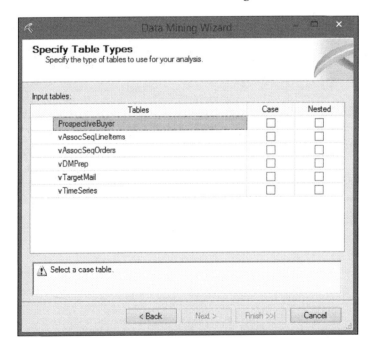

Now, we select the case table as follows:

The case table is the one that has all the cases (essentially the set of values for different attributes) required to be provided to the model for making predictions. We will also use nested tables in the upcoming models and explain the nested tables as we encounter them.

We now select the model as the predictable column, as shown here:

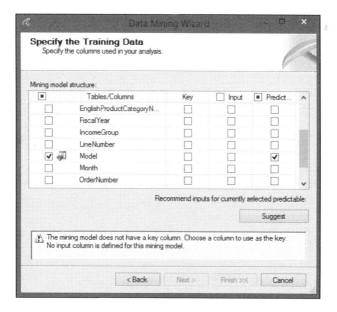

We will also select the key column (in this case, CustomerKey). We see that the **Suggest** option is now enabled. Let's click on it.

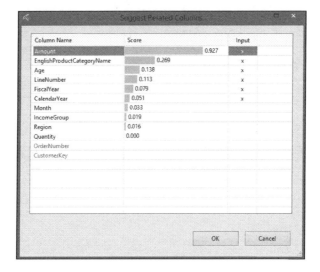

The preceding screenshot lists the columns that are closely linked with the predictable column. Thus, we see that the **Amount** column is closely related to the model, whereas **Quantity** is less so.

We click on **OK** and the input columns are automatically selected. We then click on **Next** and see that the **Content Type** and **Data Type** options are already displayed (detected) by default:

We then click on **Next** on the following screen. We specify the maximum percentage of data for the generation of the model and the maximum number of test cases, as follows:

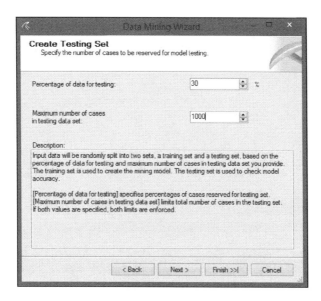

The figures are already populated by default, so we leave the default values. We now click on **Next** and then give the name for the **Mining structure name** and **Mining model name** options, as follows:

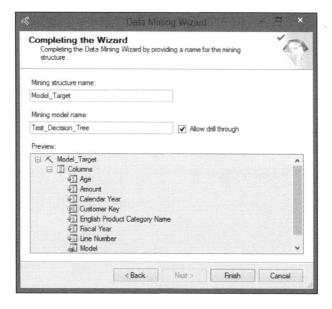

Clicking on **Finish** will lead us to the following screen:

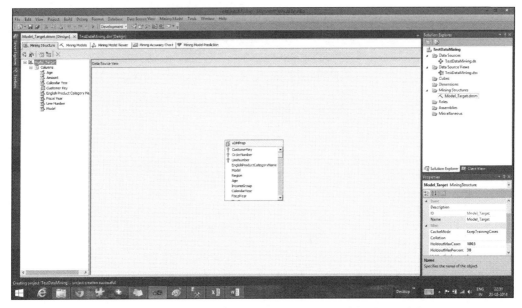

Mining Structure tab showing the view that is selected for this model

We will now process the data model by navigating to **Model_Target.dmm | Process | Run**. A detailed explanation about the processing options and settings is available in the MSDN article at `http://msdn.microsoft.com/en-us/library/ms174774.aspx`, while the MSDN article at `http://msdn.microsoft.com/en-us/library/ms176135.aspx` explains the processing requirements and considerations in detail.

Now it's time to test whether the mining model that we have created will give us a beneficial result or not. Validating and testing is an important part of the data mining process. There are three basic criteria that a data mining model should satisfy for it to be *fit* enough to be deployed in production. They are as follows:

- **Accuracy**: This refers to how accurately the model predicts the outcome with the data that has been provided
- **Reliable**: A model is said to be reliable when it predicts the outcome with the same reliability across variable data sets
- **Usefulness**: The correlation suggested by the model should aim at resolving a business problem at hand, only then we can consider the model to be useful

Testing of the model can be done by using several tools such as:

- Lift and gain chart
- Performing cross validation of data sets
- Classification matrices
- Scatter plots
- Profit charts

The MSDN article at `http://msdn.microsoft.com/en-us/library/ms175428.aspx` describes all the preceding tools in detail.

Let's use the lift chart to determine whether the mining model that we selected is really effective or not. Using the lift chart is a random selection, any other tool can also be used. Click on the **Mining Accuracy Chart** tab, and then select **Mountain-500** from **Predict Value**. We then check the **Use mining structure test cases** option to use the test data defined during the model definition, as shown in the following screenshot:

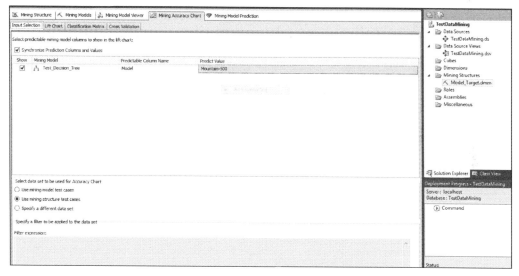

Testing the model for the product Mountain-500 model

We now click on the **Lift Chart** tab on the same screen and then check whether our model gives us the value near ideal value, as shown here:

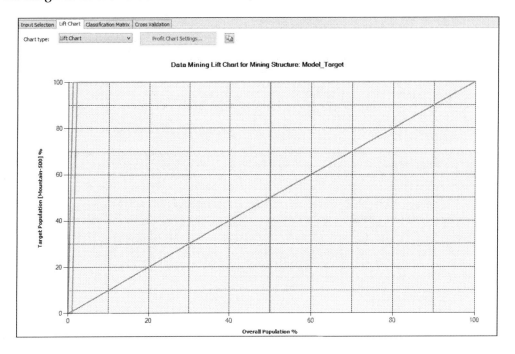

This looks promising because the lift ratio is good, as we can see in the chart, so we can go ahead and start the prediction now.

We now go to the **Mining Model Prediction** tab, select the **DMPrep** view in **Input Table**, and then select the values in the grid, as shown here:

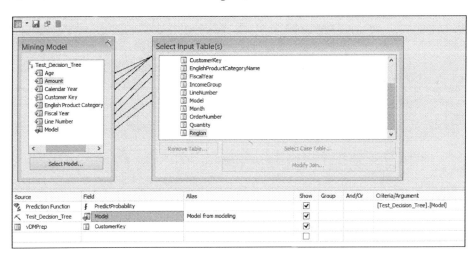

We now click on the result option at the top-left corner of the screen and get the following result:

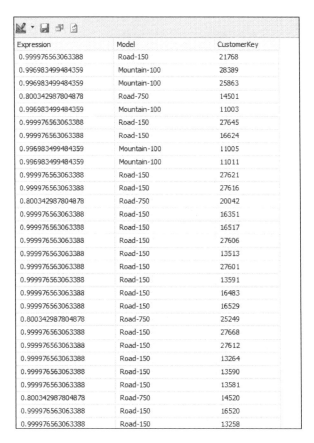

Expression	Model	CustomerKey
0.999976563063388	Road-150	21768
0.996983499484359	Mountain-100	28389
0.996983499484359	Mountain-100	25863
0.800342987804878	Road-750	14501
0.996983499484359	Mountain-100	11003
0.999976563063388	Road-150	27645
0.999976563063388	Road-150	16624
0.996983499484359	Mountain-100	11005
0.996983499484359	Mountain-100	11011
0.999976563063388	Road-150	27621
0.999976563063388	Road-150	27616
0.800342987804878	Road-750	20042
0.999976563063388	Road-150	16351
0.999976563063388	Road-150	16517
0.999976563063388	Road-150	27606
0.999976563063388	Road-150	13513
0.999976563063388	Road-150	27601
0.999976563063388	Road-150	13591
0.999976563063388	Road-150	16483
0.999976563063388	Road-150	16529
0.800342987804878	Road-750	25249
0.999976563063388	Road-150	27668
0.999976563063388	Road-150	27612
0.999976563063388	Road-150	13264
0.999976563063388	Road-150	13590
0.999976563063388	Road-150	13581
0.800342987804878	Road-750	14520
0.999976563063388	Road-150	16520
0.999976563063388	Road-150	13258

This is only a partial list but it answers most of the questions that we started out with. We can also save the list to a database table or an Excel sheet. What's more, we can add more columns from the mining model in the prediction query and predict the value for those variables accordingly.

Deploying data models

In this section, we will discuss the deployment of the data mining algorithms with their periodic updates.

Usually, we do not need to deploy the data mining models explicitly as processing and deploying is required before we perform the validation and prediction of the variable that we are interested in.

We can also explicitly deploy the data mining models by right-clicking on the model name in the **Solution Explorer** tab and then clicking on the **Process**. We will get the following screen:

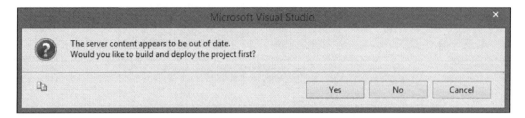

Clicking on **Yes** will deploy the project as an Analysis Services database and then we can proceed to the processing phase with the following screen:

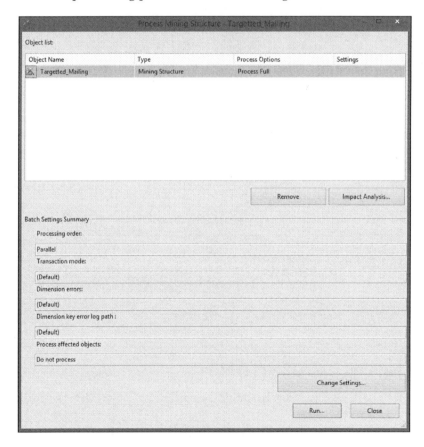

When we click on **Run**, we usually issue a full processing request. We can also select a request from other processing options by clicking on the specific option from the processing option's drop-down menu.

When the processing is complete, we will encounter a window similar to the following one:

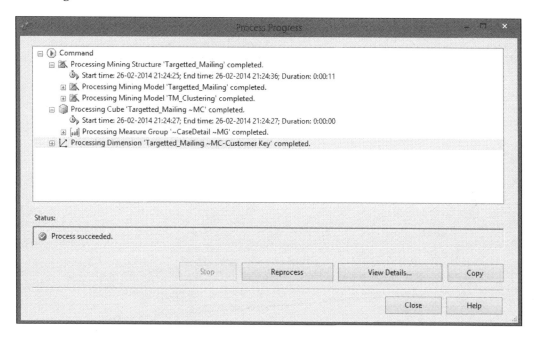

Usually, the deployment is incremental in nature, which means that if we make any changes to the model and then deploy again, only the mining model that was changed will be updated. However, if we want the entire database to be refreshed, we can set the **Deployment Mode** property accordingly.

Updating the models

The following are ways to update the models:

- **Using the SQL Server Data Tools**: This is the easiest and most straightforward way to manage the data mining models

- **Using the SQL Server Management Studio**: This provides a way to manage the data mining structures using **Data Mining Extensions (DMX)**

- **Using the Analysis Management Objects**: This is used to manage infrastructure based on **Analysis Management Objects (AMO)**

Summary

In this chapter, we covered the current market trends and business requirements for predictive data analysis, which is also called data mining. In order to deploy a successful data mining model, you need to have a clear idea of your end goal, develop a thorough understanding of the data that you are dealing with, transform and clean the data accordingly, and last but not least develop a mining algorithm. In the next chapter, we will take a look at the different tools that SQL Server offers to help develop a data mining model. The SQL Server Business Intelligence suite provides a rich set of components, which could be used at different stages of data modeling. The next chapter will focus on a few of those commonly used tools of the trade, such as SQL Server Integration Services, SQL Server Analysis Services, and SQL Server Reporting Services.

3
Tools of the Trade

Data mining as a process is closely dependent on the knowledge of the entire SQL Server BI Suite. The SQL Server BI Suite provides the tools that are important at the stage of the data mining process. The data mining process consists of activities such as hosting the data generated from different business processes (in the form of SQL Server tables), designing the data warehouse project (with the help of SQL Server Data Tools), which will contain the historical data of different departments of the organization, hosting the data marts that could be in the form of relational databases or cubes and giving a visualization on the data (in the form of SQL Server reports). Thus, we will devote this chapter to take a tour of the important components of the SQL Server BI Suite, which are SQL Server Integration Services, SQL Server Analysis Services, and SQL Server Reporting Services. This chapter should not be considered as a deep dive but rather a refresher and walkthrough on the various tools of the SQL Server BI Suite.

In this chapter, we will cover the following topics:

- SQL Server BI Suite
- SQL Server 2014
    - Integration services
    - Analysis services
    - Reporting services

SQL Server BI Suite

The SQL Server BI Suite encompasses the entire range of tools and applications that are available out of the box along with the SQL Server installation. The following list highlights some of these tools and applications:

- **SQL Server Engine**: This is the core service preliminarily used to store, process, and secure data
- **SQL Server Data Tools**: This is an **Integrated Development Environment (IDE)** to design and develop solutions for the SQL Server platform both on and off premises
- **SQL Server Analysis Services**: This service provides **Online Application Processing (OLAP)** and data mining capabilities to the users
- **SQL Server Integration Services**: This service provides the enterprise-level extract, transform, and load capabilities to the users
- **SQL Server Data Quality Services**: This tool provides the ability to maintain data quality and ensures that the data is suitable for business usage
- **SQL Server Reporting Services**: This is an out-of-box reporting tool that provides the end user with enterprise-level reporting capabilities
- **SQL Server Master Data Services**: This is a solution from Microsoft to solve the problem of Master Data Management for the enterprise

We will now describe each one of them and touch the base on any new features included in SQL Server 2014.

SQL Server Engine

This is the service that provides the storing, processing, and securing of data. We can create relational databases and the databases for online analytical processing, and access the data from our application in a controlled manner. We can also apply transformations, apply suitable techniques for faster data access, or execute SQL queries using the **SQL Server Management Studio (SSMS)**.

SQL Server 2014 brings a host of changes in the following areas:

- Memory-optimized tables
- Ability to handle SQL Server data files on Windows Azure
- Some backup and restore enhancements
- AlwaysOn enhancements
- Enhancements at the **Transact-SQL (TSQL)** and system views
- Clustered column store indexes

The MSDN article at `http://technet.microsoft.com/en-us/library/bb510411.aspx` provides a complete list of changes that are packaged with SQL Server 2014. Knowing about these changes will help us use these features when we are dealing with the data that originates from different sources and is of varying complexities. Employing these features can help faster and efficient access to data.

SQL Server Data Tools

Formerly known as **Business Intelligence Development Studio (BIDS)**, SQL Server Data Tools is the most important and perhaps the only tool that is majorly used by **Business Intelligence (BI)** developers to develop any projects, be it an Analysis Services project, the data mining project, an Integration Services Project, or a Reporting Services Project.

Starting 2014, the SQL Server Data Tools has the connector for **Parallel Data Warehouse (PDW)** as shown here:

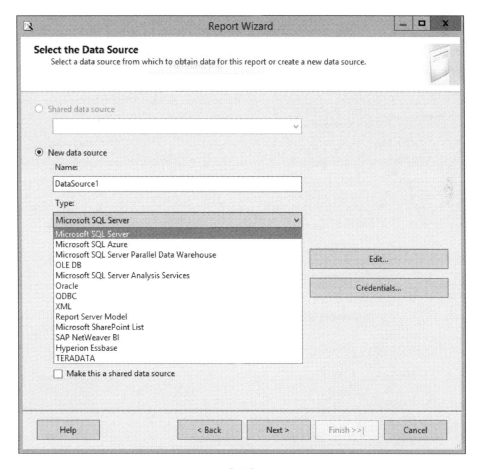

SQL Server Data Quality Services

SQL Server Data Quality Services helps a BI developer to filter the data that is inward bound to the staging database or the data warehouse database. We have already worked with Data Quality Services to filter our data in *Chapter 1, Identifying, Staging, and Understanding Data*, and had experienced some of its benefits.

In SQL Server 2014, there are no changes in the functionality of the Data Quality Services.

SQL Server Integration Services

When we encounter a need to pump the data from the staging database into the data warehouse, Integration Services is our best tool of choice. It is the ETL platform that lets us pull data from different data sources, define the data transformation and data profiling tasks, and many other data transformation and transferring capabilities. We will now try to load the sample data into the warehouse from the AdventureWorks2014 OLTP database.

Let's now create a sample Integration Services project to transfer the data from the AdventureWorks2014 OLTP database to the AdventureWorks2014 DW database. Let's take a look at the schema of the Employee table:

```
[BusinessEntityID]
[NationalIDNumber]
[LoginID]
[OrganizationNode]
[OrganizationLevel]
[JobTitle]
[BirthDate]
[MaritalStatus]
[Gender]
[HireDate]
[SalariedFlag]
[VacationHours]
[SickLeaveHours]
[CurrentFlag]
[rowguid]
[ModifiedDate]
```

The following is the `DimEmployee` table in the AdventureWorks2014DW database:

```
[EmployeeKey]
[ParentEmployeeKey]
[EmployeeNationalIDAlternateKey]
[ParentEmployeeNationalIDAlternateKey]
[SalesTerritoryKey]
[FirstName]
[LastName]
[MiddleName]
[NameStyle]
[Title]
[HireDate]
[BirthDate]
[LoginID]
[EmailAddress]
[Phone]
[MaritalStatus]
[EmergencyContactName]
[EmergencyContactPhone]
[SalariedFlag]
[Gender]
[PayFrequency]
[BaseRate]
[VacationHours]
[SickLeaveHours]
[CurrentFlag]
[SalesPersonFlag]
[DepartmentName]
[StartDate] Logind
[EndDate]
[Status]
[EmployeePhoto]
```

It is quite evident that the DimEmployee table has much more information about an employee. This is due to the way in which we design the dimensions, that is, by grouping all the attributes together. It will be technically incorrect to say that a Dimension table is a deformalized table. This additional information has to be sourced from other tables in the AdventureWorks database. Let's examine the tables that will give us the information we require and list the values that we will get from the Employee table, as shown in the following diagram:

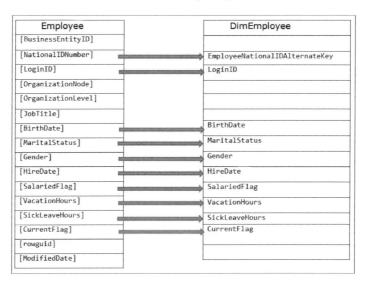

Now, we will look at the **Department** table in the AdventureWorks2014 database, which has the following columns:

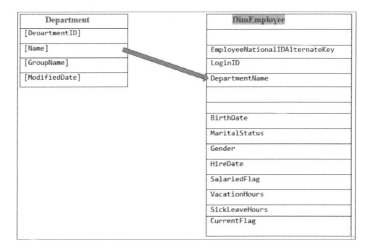

Next, we will look at the `EmployeePayHistory` table in the AdventureWorks2014 database, which has the following columns:

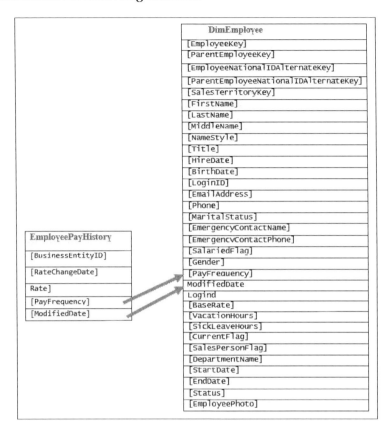

Take a look at the `EmployeeDepartmentHistory` table in the AdventureWorks2014 database, which has the following columns:

DimEmployee
[EmployeeKey]
[ParentEmployeeKey]
[EmployeeNationalIDAlternateKey]
[ParentEmployeeNationalIDAlternateKey]
[SalesTerritoryKey]
[FirstName]
[LastName]
[MiddleName]
[NameStyle]
[Title]
[HireDate]
[BirthDate]
[LoginID]
[EmailAddress]
[Phone]
[MaritalStatus]
[EmergencyContactName]
[EmergencyContactPhone]
[SalariedFlag]
[Gender]
[PayFrequency]
ModifiedDate
LogInd
[BaseRate]
[VacationHours]
[SickLeaveHours]
[CurrentFlag]
[SalesPersonFlag]
[DepartmentName]
[StartDate]
[EndDate]
[Status]
[EmployeePhoto]

EmployeeDepartmentHistory
[BusinessEntityID]
[DepartmentID]
[ShiftID]
[StartDate]
[EndDate]
[ModifiedDate]

We'll now look at the `Person` table in the AdventureWorks2014 database, which has the following columns:

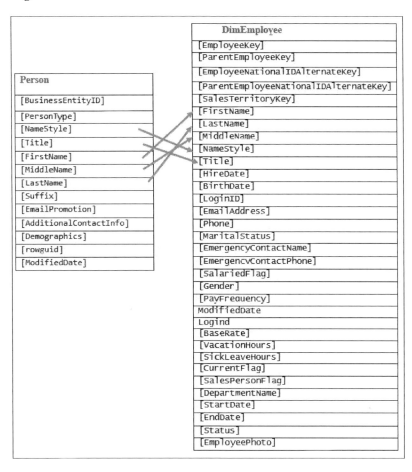

Let's look at the `EmailAddress` table in the AdventureWorks2014 database, which has the following columns:

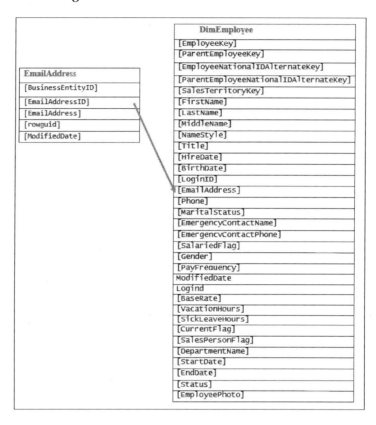

Finally, see the `SalesPerson` table in the AdventureWorks2014 database, which has the following columns:

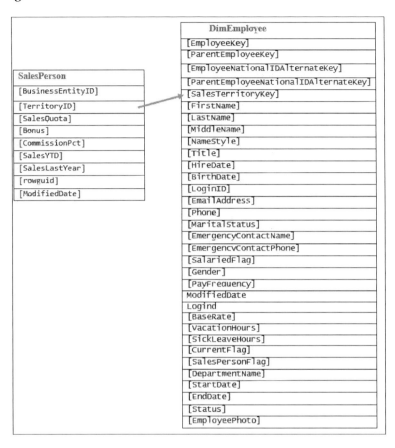

If we create a dimension for sales with the `SalesPerson` and `SalesTerritory` table, we will get the value of `SalesTerritoryKey`. The `EmployeeKey` column will be a `SurrogateKey` column that we will generate.

The values that are missing (which cannot be mapped to any of the other tables) are as follows:

- `[ParentEmployeeKey]`: This is the value from the `EmployeeKey` column of the `DimEmployee` table

- `[EmployeeNationalIDAlternateKey]`: This is the value of the `NationalID` column of `DimEmployee table.emp`

- `[ParentEmployeeNationalIDAlternateKey]`: This is the value of the `ForeignKey` column of the `DimEmployee` table

Let's now get the Integration Services package to transfer the data from the `Employee` table to the `DimEmployee` table. For the current example, we will ignore the `ParentEmployeeKey`, `EmployeeNationalIDAlternateKey`, and `ParentEmployeeNationalIDAlternateKey` columns.

1. Open up SQL Server Data Tools and select the **Integration Services Project**. Then, store it in the folder at `C:\TransferProject\`, as shown in the following screenshot:

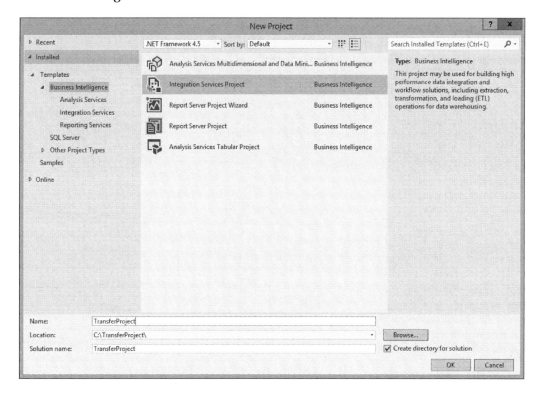

2. Select the **ADO.NET** connection manager type, as shown in the following screenshot. We can also use other data sources such as **OLEDB**, **ODBC**, and so on. But of course, we will have to configure the connection managers appropriately and make sure we have the DSN's set up.

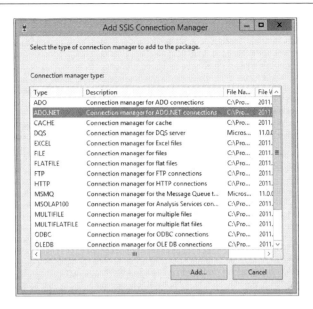

3. Click on **Add** and then **New** to open the **Connection Manager** dialog box and then type . in the **Server name** textbox and AdventureWorks2014 in the **Database name** textbox, as shown in the following screenshot. This means that the server is present on the machine where you are developing the SSIS solution.

4. Click on **OK** twice to save, and exit the **Connection Manager** dialog box. For our example of pulling up the majority of rows for the `DimEmployee` table, we can end up with the following statement:

```
with employee_cte
(EmployeeNationalIDAlternateKey,LoginID,BirthDate,
MaritalStatus, Gender,HireDate,SalariedFlag,VacationHours,SickLeav
eHours,
CurrentFlag,DepartmentName,PayFrequency,ModifiedDate,
StartDate, EndDate,NameStyle,Title,FirstName,MiddleName,
LastName,EmailAddress)
as
(
    select e.NationalIDNumber as
EmployeeNationalIDAlternateKey,LoginID,BirthDate,MaritalStatus,
Gender,HireDate,SalariedFlag,VacationHours,SickLeaveHours,
CurrentFlag,d.Name as DepartmentName,PayFrequency,e.
ModifiedDate,StartDate,EndDate,
NameStyle,
    Title,FirstName,MiddleName,LastName,EmailAddress from
        [HumanResources].[Employee]
    e,[HumanResources].[Department] d,
        [HumanResources].[EmployeePayHistory] eph,[Person].[Person]
    p,
     [Person].[EmailAddress]
     ea,[HumanResources].[EmployeeDepartmentHistory] edh
    where
        e.BusinessEntityID=eph.BusinessEntityID
        and e.BusinessEntityID=edh.BusinessEntityID
        and edh.departmentid=d.DepartmentID
        and e.BusinessEntityID=p.BusinessEntityID
        and e.BusinessEntityID=ea.BusinessEntityID
)

select * from employee_cte;
```

We use the common table expressions here even though it might just behave like a normal view, it is not stored in the database as an object. Moreover, it can be used to make changes to the underlying data just like a normal view. Now let's include this statement in a SQL Server Integration Services Package. The following screenshot shows the settings for the source in the data flow tasks:

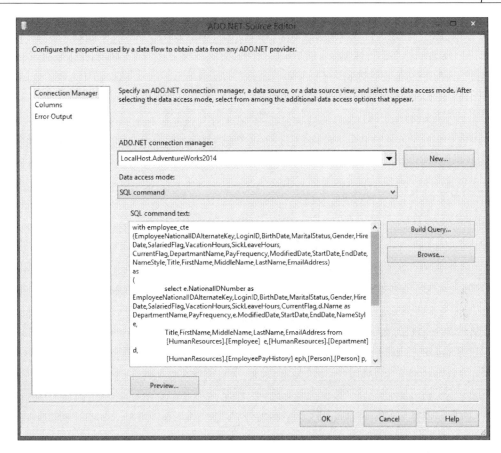

The **Data Flow** task will be a very simple one consisting of a source and a destination, as shown in the following screenshot:

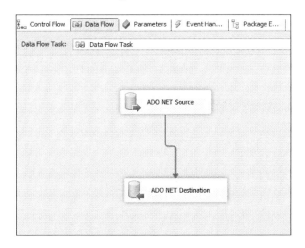

Testing of the package can be done by using the SSIS Tester available for download at `https://www.nuget.org/packages/SSISTester/2.0.0-b152`. Alternatively, we can execute the package against a smaller subset of data to see whether the outcome obtained is as desired or not.

SQL Server Analysis Services

Now that we have the data into the data warehouse database, we now need to get the data mart ready. Let's create the Analysis Services Project, as shown here:

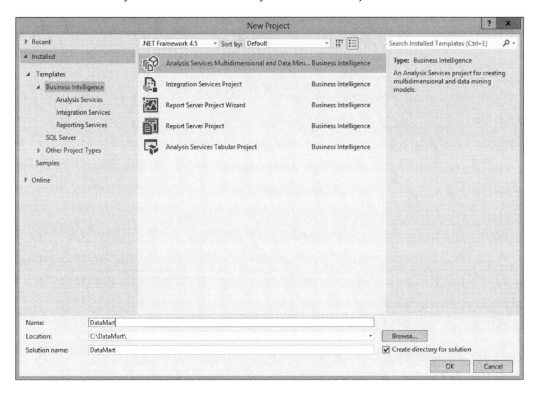

The next step is to create a connection with the database. To do this, follow these steps:

1. Type . in the **Server name** textbox and `AdventureWorksDW2014` in the **Select or enter a database name** textbox, as shown in the following screenshot:

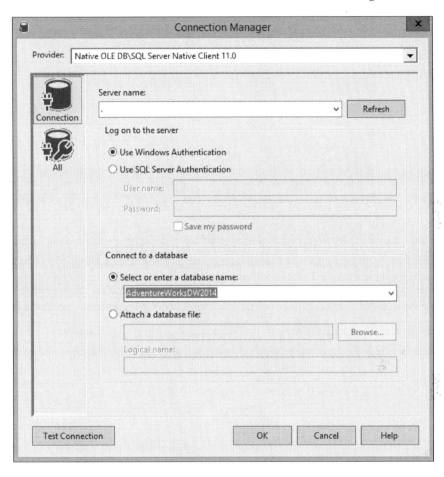

2. Click on **Next** and then select the **Use the service account** option for **Impersonation Information,** as shown here:

3. Click on **Next** and then click on **Finish**.

Let's now create the **Data Source View Wizard**. To do this, follows these steps:

1. First we select the DimEmployee table, as shown here:

2. Add all the other related tables that we will need to build the entire model by clicking on the **Add Related Tables** button, as shown in the following screenshot:

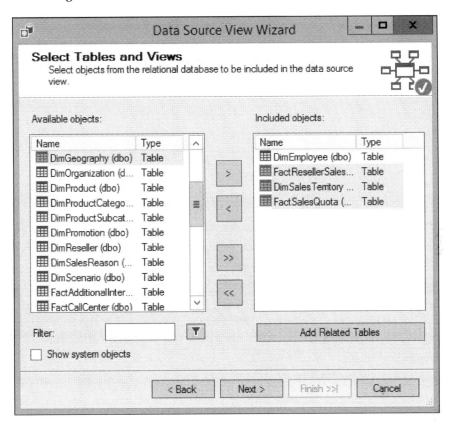

3. Complete the preceding wizard by clicking on **Next** and then on **Finish**. We will now obtain the resultant data source view, as shown here:

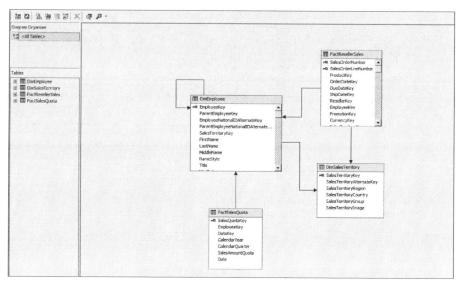

DataSource view consisting of DimEmployee , FactInternetSales, FactSalesQuota, and the DimSalesTerritory tables

4. Now, let's create a cube by right-clicking on **Cubes** and starting the **Cube Wizard** dialog box. Then, select the **Use existing tables** option, as shown here:

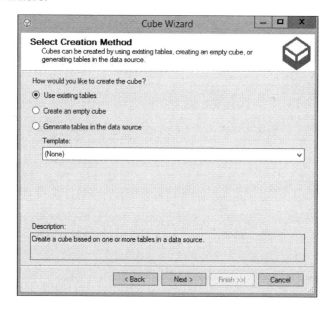

5. We now click on **Next** and then select all the measure groups, as shown in the following screenshot:

6. Click on **Next** and then on **Finish** to get the cube and the dimensions. Right-click on the **DataMart** database and then click on **Deploy**. We will be presented with the following dialog box that shows the progress of the deployment:

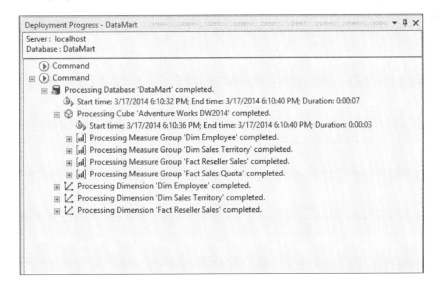

After completion of the deployment, we will see the cube deployed on the server, as shown here:

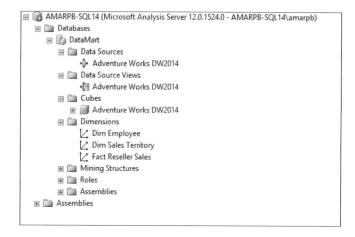

SQL Server Reporting Services

Let's now create a report with the help of the SQL Server Reporting Services. We need to select a new project and then select the **Report Server Project** type, as shown in the following screenshot:

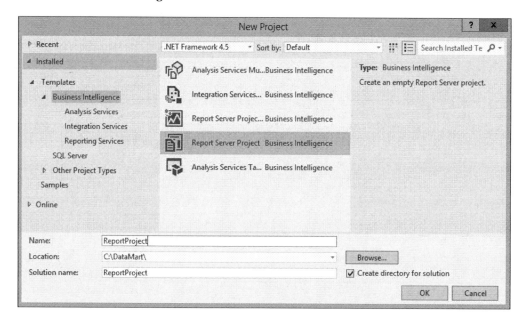

We then need to create the following data source for the report:

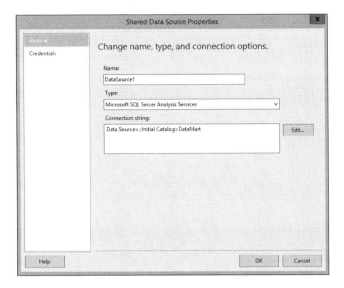

Let's now create a report and design a query for the **DataMart** database, as shown here:

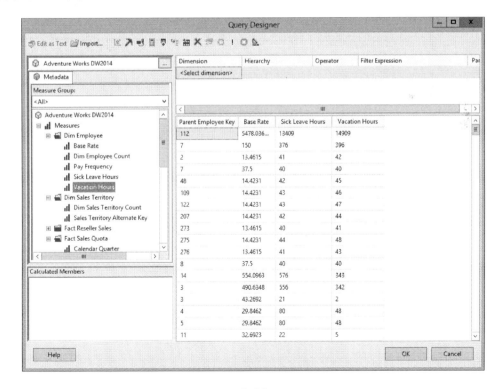

Add a table to the report and drag the four columns onto the table, as shown in the following screenshot:

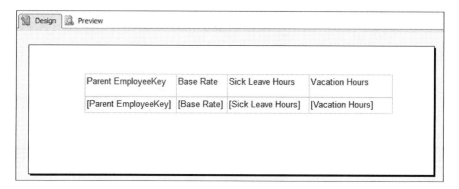

We will see the following report by clicking on the **Preview** button:

Parent Employee Key	Base Rate	Sick Leave Hours	Vacation Hours
112	5478.03679999 999	13409	14909
7	150	376	396
2	13.4615	41	42
7	37.5	40	40
48	14.4231	42	45
109	14.4231	43	46
122	14.4231	43	47
207	14.4231	42	44
273	13.4615	40	41
275	14.4231	44	48
276	13.4615	41	43
8	37.5	40	40
14	554.0963	576	343
3	490.6348	556	342
3	43.2692	21	2
4	29.8462	80	48
5	29.8462	80	48
11	32.6923	22	5
13	32.6923	23	6

References

The following are some references for the concepts covered in this chapter:

- Microsoft SQL Server at `http://msdn.microsoft.com/en-us/library/ms187875.aspx`

- Microsoft SQL Server Reporting Services at `http://msdn.microsoft.com/en-us/library/ms159106.aspx`

- Microsoft SQL Server Analysis Services at `http://msdn.microsoft.com/en-us/library/bb522607.aspx`

- Microsoft SQL Server Integration Services at `http://msdn.microsoft.com/en-us/library/ms141026.aspx`

- Microsoft SQL Server Data Quality Services at `http://msdn.microsoft.com/en-us/library/ff877925.aspx`

Summary

In this chapter, we looked at the tools that we used to create a data warehouse, followed by designing an SSIS Package to transfer data from the staging table to the data warehouse table. We also created a data mart and then created a report based on it, thus covering the entire spectrum of Business Intelligence from data gathering to data analysis. This process is followed when we build the enterprise reporting, and the knowledge of the tools and tricks used at various stages will be useful as we proceed further in the book.

4
Preparing the Data

In the previous chapter, we got acquainted with the tools that we'll use in this chapter to build our data warehouse. It is not guaranteed that we will have data from only one data source. Different departments in an enterprise environment can have different data sources and hence, the methodologies of pulling relevant data from these data sources would differ. In this chapter, we will be looking at the common data sources available to store the live data and how we can extract the data from these data sources into a common SQL Server database, which will be our staging database.

In this chapter, we will cover the following topics:

- Listing of popular databases
- Migrating data from popular databases to a staging database
- Building a data warehouse:
    - Identifying measures and facts
    - Automating data ingestion

Listing of popular databases

A data store is the most basic necessity of any application. If we are generating some data in any application, we will require a backend database for it. Various applications might entail some needs, which would require us to use some specific data sources. For example, if our host operating system is on Unix, we might go for Oracle or any of the databases that are installable on a Unix system to host our data. The following are some common enterprise data stores that are available today:

- SQL Server
- Oracle
- IBM DB2

- Sybase
- MySQL
- PostgreSQL
- Teradata
- Informix
- Ingres
- Amazon SimpleDB

We will now look at the tools available at our disposal to transfer the data from some (Oracle and IBM DB2) of the preceding database systems to SQL Server, as that is where our staging database is going to be. As discussed in the previous chapters, the same data in different applications might be represented in different forms; for example, an employee might be uniquely identified by an employee ID in the HR department but represented as an entity ID in the IT department. Therefore, we need to bring all the data together so that the data makes sense with a consistent look.

Migrating data from popular databases to a staging database

To migrate data from Oracle, we will start our discussion with the Oracle database engine and see how we can transfer the data that is hosted on the Oracle database to a table in SQL Server, and Microsoft does provide us with **SQL Server Migration Assistant (SSMA)**, which we can use to seamlessly and effortlessly transfer the data from Oracle to SQL Server.

To use the SSMA, we need to install SSMA for Oracle from `http://www.microsoft.com/en-in/download/details.aspx?id=42655`. All the versions of the Oracle client v9.0 and higher are supported.

Let's go through the process of downloading the SSMA and then migrate a table in Oracle to SQL Server:

1. After we download the ZIP folder and extract it in our local directory, we will see the following two files:

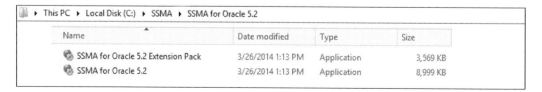

2. Double-click on the SSMA file for Oracle v5.2, click on **Run**, and then on **Next** in the resultant dialog box, as shown in the following screenshot:

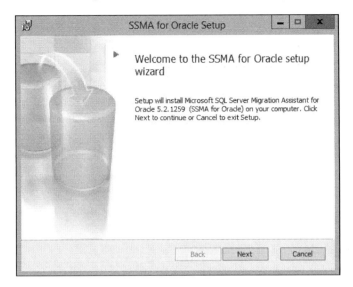

3. Now look at the following screenshot, which tells us that the Oracle client software is not found on the machine where we are installing SSMA:

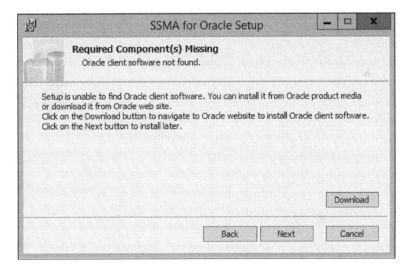

4. We will definitely require the Oracle client software so let's click on the **Download** button. We will be redirected to the Oracle website `www.oracle.com/technetwork/database/enterprise-edition/downloads/112010-win64soft-094461.html` and we get an option to download the client, as shown here:

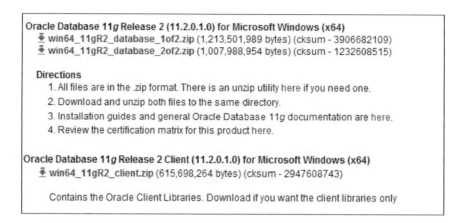

5. We need to complete the installation of the Oracle client before we can use SSMA to migrate the data. We then click on **Next** and accept the license agreement. Click on **Next** again and select **Complete** in the set-up option, as shown in the following screenshot:

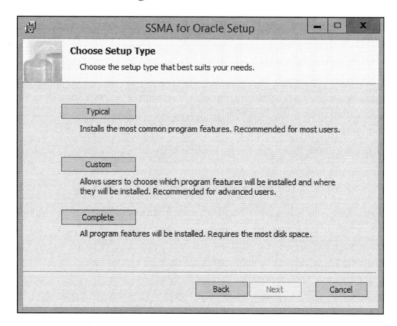

6. We will be prompted for the installation in the next screen, which we need to accept and proceed with the installation. On successful completion, we will get the following message:

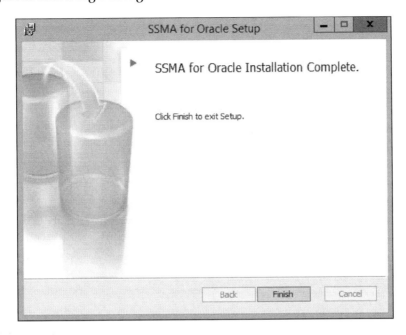

7. We then start the SQL Server Migration Assistant which prompts us for the **License Key**, as shown here:

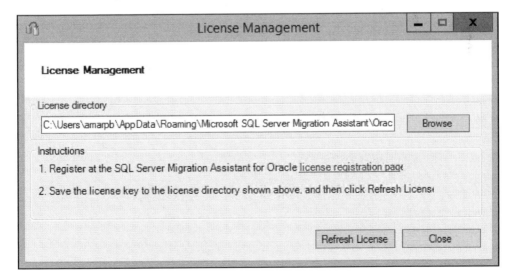

8. When we click on the license registration page link, we are redirected to `http://www.microsoft.com/en-us/download/details.aspx?id=40911` from where we can download the license files. Name the license file `oracle-ssma.license`. Then, copy this file to the directory mentioned in the preceding screenshot and click on the **Refresh License** button. If the license key is accepted, we will get the following message box:

9. We then click on **OK**, and the following SSMA screen opens up automatically:

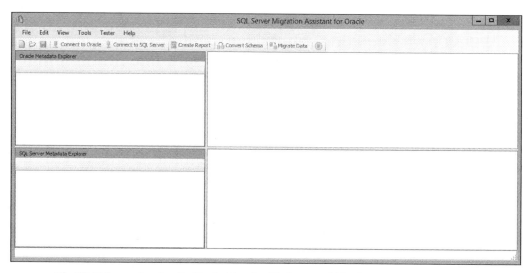

The SSMA home showing the Oracle Metadata Explorer and SQL Server Metadata Explorer

10. We now click on **File** and select **New Project**. We can now see that we have the **Connect to Oracle** option available. On clicking on the **Connect to Oracle** option, we will see the following connection dialog box:

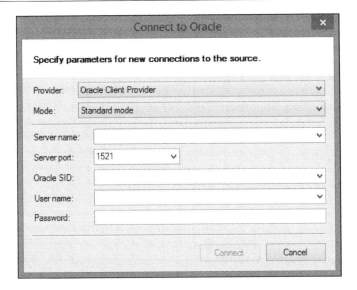

11. We can leave the **Provider** option to default **Oracle Client Provider**. We now select **TNSNAME mode** in the **Mode** option and enter the values in the **Connection identifier**, **User name**, and **Password** fields, as shown here:

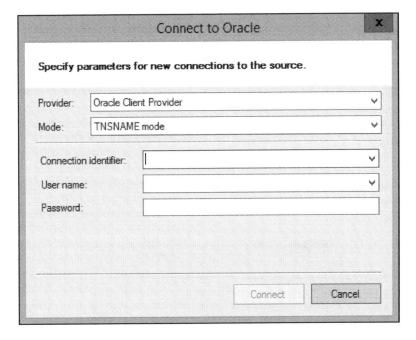

12. After this, we will see the objects that are being loaded in the UI as well as its status at the bottom of the UI, as shown in the following screenshot:

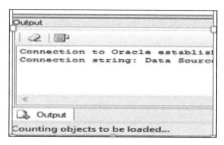

Status of the connection to the Oracle database, the connection string, and the current operation being performed

To be able to connect to the SQL Server instance, we have to install the SSMA for Oracle v5.2 Extension Pack and have to ensure that the SQL Server Agent Service is running; further details are available at `http://technet.microsoft.com/en-us/library/hh313165.aspx`.

1. When we connect to the SQL Server instance, we will see the following screenshot:

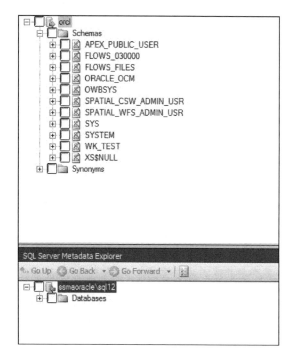

2. We then select the tables that we need to migrate, as shown here:

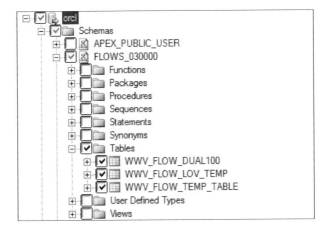

3. Click on **Convert Schema** and allow the wizard to finish. We will see the database FLOWS_030000 added to the SQL Server tree, as shown in the following screenshot:

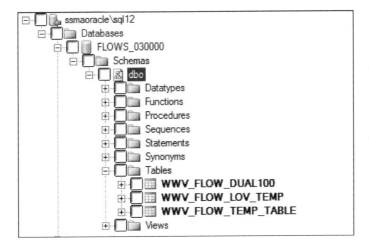

4. Right-click on `FLOWS_030000` and then click on the **Save as Script** option. Save the script for the creation of the database objects, as shown here:

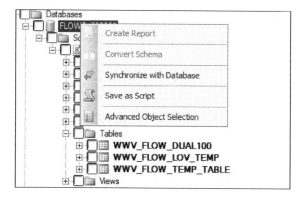

5. We now open the SQL Server Management Studio, open the saved script, and then execute the script on the `FLOWS_030000`, as shown in the following screenshot:

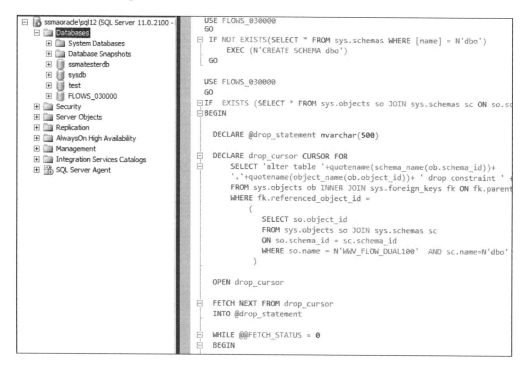

6. We now go back to the SSMA and then click on the **Migrate Data** option, as shown here:

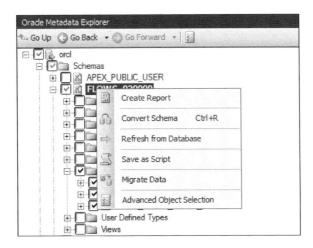

7. We will be prompted for the credentials and then the data migration will begin. After the migration is completed successfully, we will see the following report:

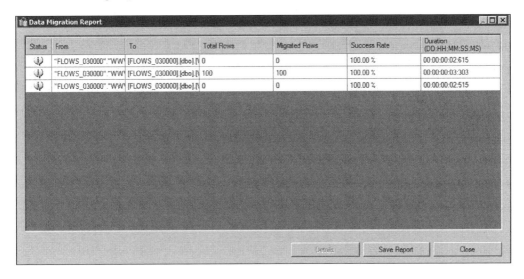

The link at `http://technet.microsoft.com/en-us/library/hh313155.aspx` also provides other options that we can use while migrating the data.

We could also use the Integration Services to transfer the data but that would require us to install Attunity drivers, which are available only for the Enterprise or Developers edition customers; SSMA does not have such constraints.

Migrating data from IBM DB2

IBM DB2 is a major data storage in many organizations and therefore the inclusion of a scenario of transferring data from IBM DB2 to SQL Server is no surprise. SQL Server Integration Services make the entire process of transferring data from IBM DB2 to SQL Server a piece of cake, as you will see.

Let's consider an example wherein we have a sample database on the IBM DB2 database instance:

1. Let's list **Active Databases**, as shown in the following screenshot:

```
db2 => list active databases

                        Active Databases

Database name                          = SAMPLE
Applications connected currently       = 1
Database path                          = C:\DB2\NODE0000\SQL00001\MEMBER0000
\

db2 =>
```

2. Next, let's list the tables in the database sample, as shown here:

```
db2 => list tables

Table/View          Schema       Type  Creation time
                    --------     ----  -------------
ACT                 AMARPB       T     2014-04-02-04.28.22.022011
ADEFUSR             AMARPB       S     2014-04-02-04.28.32.037002
CATALOG             AMARPB       T     2014-04-02-04.28.55.068002
CL_SCHED            AMARPB       T     2014-04-02-04.28.15.772001
CUSTOMER            AMARPB       T     2014-04-02-04.28.51.724002
DEPARTMENT          AMARPB       T     2014-04-02-04.28.16.882002
DEPT                AMARPB       A     2014-04-02-04.28.17.920000
EMP                 AMARPB       A     2014-04-02-04.28.18.803003
EMPACT              AMARPB       A     2014-04-02-04.28.22.022004
EMPLOYEE            AMARPB       T     2014-04-02-04.28.17.928003
EMPMDC              AMARPB       T     2014-04-02-04.28.36.225001
EMPPROJACT          AMARPB       T     2014-04-02-04.28.21.647002
EMP_ACT             AMARPB       A     2014-04-02-04.28.22.022008
EMP_PHOTO           AMARPB       T     2014-04-02-04.28.18.803006
EMP_RESUME          AMARPB       T     2014-04-02-04.28.19.710001
INVENTORY           AMARPB       T     2014-04-02-04.28.50.646002
IN_TRAY             AMARPB       T     2014-04-02-04.28.22.413002
ORG                 AMARPB       T     2014-04-02-04.28.22.553002
PRODUCT             AMARPB       T     2014-04-02-04.28.40.115001
PRODUCTSUPPLIER     AMARPB       T     2014-04-02-04.28.50.131007
PROJ                AMARPB       A     2014-04-02-04.28.21.225003
PROJACT             AMARPB       T     2014-04-02-04.28.21.225006
PROJECT             AMARPB       T     2014-04-02-04.28.20.522004
PURCHASEORDER       AMARPB       T     2014-04-02-04.28.53.506004
```

3. We will now list the records in the department table, as shown in the following screenshot:

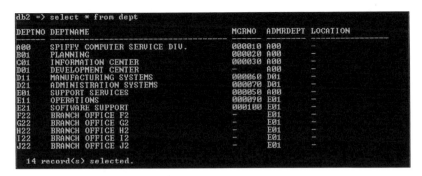

4. We will now try to transfer these records with the help of an SSIS package to a SQL Server database. We will first have to download the Microsoft OLEDB provider for DB2 from `http://www.microsoft.com/en-us/download/details.aspx?id=35580`. We can download the `DB2OLEDBV4_X64` or `DB2OLEDBV4_X86` binaries according to our requirements.

5. Here, we installed the `DB2OLEDBV4_X64` binary and then tried to create a connection to the `SAMPLE DB2` database using the OLEDB provider, as shown here:

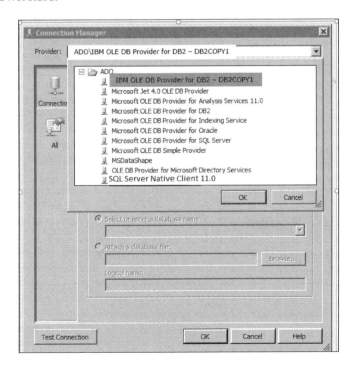

6. We then create the **Data Flow Task**, as shown in the following screenshot:

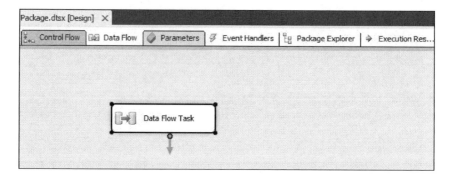

7. We now add the OLE DB source with the properties, as shown here:

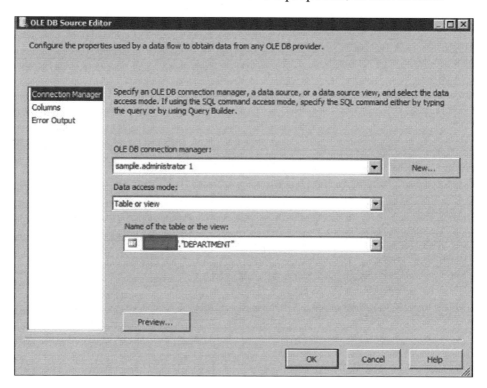

Before proceeding ahead, let's create the table in the target database. For this, we will use the following `create` statement:

```
Create table Department(
Deptno          varchar(3),
Deptname    varchar(36),
Mgrno           varchar(6),
Admrdept    varchar(3),
Location    varchar(16)
)
```

Now, let's add **SQL Destination** with properties, as shown in the following screenshot. The SQL Server instance name is `db2test` and the database name is `IBMDB2`.

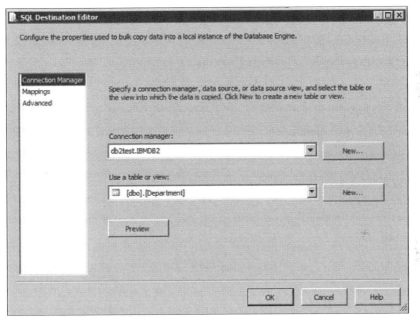

Specifying the name of the connection manager, the database object being accessed, and the name of the table or view

We will now execute the package. We won't go further to show how to execute the package as the execution of the package has been covered in *Chapter 3, Tools of the Trade*.

Building a data warehouse

Identification of dimensions and measures is one of the most preliminary operations that have to be performed before we can have a data warehouse database, on which we can perform a data mining operation. The identification of dimensions and measures are important as they will help you group together the data corresponding to similar functionality. Examples can be customer, sales, finance, employee, and so on. Dimensions and facts corresponding to the employee aims at providing you with all the information corresponding to an employee of the organization, while dimensions and facts corresponding to a customer aims at providing you with complete customer details. For more information on measure and measure groups, refer to the Microsoft article at `http://technet.microsoft.com/en-us/library/ms174792(v=sql.90).aspx` and the article at `http://technet.microsoft.com/en-us/library/ms175669(v=sql.90).aspx`, which talks about the dimension relationships. Let's now study the AdventureWorksDW2014 database and see how the data has been grouped together. This understanding will help you design the tables on which we will perform the data mining operation.

Let's look at the `DimEmployee` table that has the following columns:

```
[EmployeeKey]
    ,[ParentEmployeeKey]
    ,[EmployeeNationalIDAlternateKey]
    ,[ParentEmployeeNationalIDAlternateKey]
    ,[SalesTerritoryKey]
    ,[FirstName]
    ,[LastName]
    ,[MiddleName]
    ,[NameStyle]
    ,[Title]
    ,[HireDate]
    ,[BirthDate]
    ,[LoginID]
    ,[EmailAddress]
    ,[Phone]
    ,[MaritalStatus]
    ,[EmergencyContactName]
    ,[EmergencyContactPhone]
    ,[SalariedFlag]
    ,[Gender]
    ,[PayFrequency]
    ,[BaseRate]
    ,[VacationHours]
    ,[SickLeaveHours]
    ,[CurrentFlag]
    ,[SalesPersonFlag]
    ,[DepartmentName]
```

```
, [StartDate]
, [EndDate]
, [Status]
, [EmployeePhoto]
```

If we look closely at this table, we will see a foreign-key relationship in the form of the `SalesTerritory` key; also, there are no further relationships defined. This gives us an indication that the dimension employee has been designed keeping in mind the sales of the organization; if we take a look at each and every dimension, we will see that they are targeted towards giving us a better insight into the sales of the organization or they are directed towards giving us some information about the financial status of the organization.

Now, consider a situation wherein we want to do some predictive analysis on an employee of the organization. Let's suppose that we want to understand how the career profile of employees looks like, for example, how the employees having a common set of family or financial backgrounds or having a common set of educational backgrounds tend to advance them in their career. We will not be able to design a data mining model for the preceding scenario based on the design of the AdventureWorksDW database. We will probably have to redesign the dimensions and facts to enable data mining for the employee data.

We now look at the table and views that are of interest to us in the current AdventureWorksDW database, namely, `ProspectiveBuyer`, and the views `vAssocSeqLineItems`, `vAssocSeqOrders`, `vTargetMail`, and `vTimeSeries`, and would try to set up a periodical data load into these tables based on their dependencies.

The data load can be fully refreshed wherein all the data from the beginning of time is loaded into the table after the old data is deleted, or it can be an incremental load wherein only the change in the data is loaded.

We have already seen how we can load data from the AdventureWorks OLTP database to the AdventureWorksDW database; the `ProspectiveBuyer` table can be loaded directly from the OLTP database while the views are loaded from the facts and dimensions of the DW database. We will try to incrementally load the `ProspectiveBuyer` table from the `DimCustomer` table in the AdventureWorksDW database using SSIS in the next section.

Let's set up a framework to incrementally load the data corresponding to `vTargetMail`. Since it is a view, we don't worry about the incremental loading of the data but if we do have `TargetMail` as a table, we would want to have a strategy in place for the incremental or delta load operations.

Automating data ingestion

The following columns belong to the `ProspectiveBuyer` table:

```
[ProspectiveBuyerKey]
, [ProspectAlternateKey]
      , [FirstName]
      , [MiddleName]
      , [LastName]
      , [BirthDate]
      , [MaritalStatus]
      , [Gender]
      , [EmailAddress]
      , [YearlyIncome]
      , [TotalChildren]
      , [NumberChildrenAtHome]
      , [Education]
      , [Occupation]
      , [HouseOwnerFlag]
      , [NumberCarsOwned]
      , [AddressLine1]
      , [AddressLine2]
      , [City]
      , [StateProvinceCode]
      , [PostalCode]
      , [Phone]
      , [Salutation]
      , [Unknown]
```

Let's try to understand the mapping of the `ProspectiveBuyer` table with the `DimCustomer` table. The following are the columns of the `DimCustomer` table:

```
      [CustomerKey]
, [GeographyKey]
, [CustomerAlternateKey]
, [Title]
, [FirstName]
, [MiddleName]
, [LastName]
, [NameStyle]
, [BirthDate]
, [MaritalStatus]
, [Suffix]
, [Gender]
, [EmailAddress]
, [YearlyIncome]
, [TotalChildren]
, [NumberChildrenAtHome]
, [EnglishEducation]
, [SpanishEducation]
```

```
, [FrenchEducation]
, [EnglishOccupation]
, [SpanishOccupation]
, [FrenchOccupation]
, [HouseOwnerFlag]
, [NumberCarsOwned]
, [AddressLine1]
, [AddressLine2]
, [Phone]
, [DateFirstPurchase]
, [CommuteDistance]
```

By comparing the two tables, we can see that most of the columns in the
ProspectiveBuyer table derive their data from the DimCustomer table, so we
will create a package to incrementally load the ProspectiveBuyer table. In order
to check whether a new record does exist in the ProspectiveBuyer table, we
need to have a column that will decide the uniqueness of the row in the table. By
straight observation, we conclude that EmailAddress is the only field that suits our
requirement of the unique column.

We will now create an SSIS package for the incremental load. For this, we create a
new package and then create a new ADO.NET connection manager, as shown in the
following screenshot:

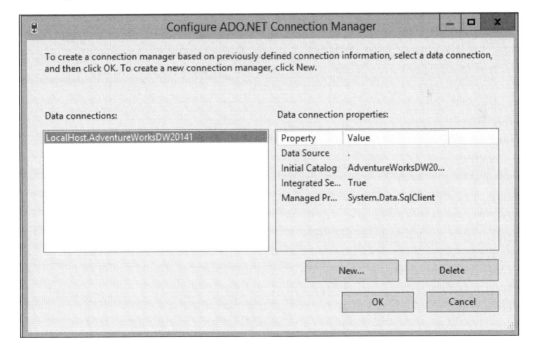

Change the connection type and the connection properties so that it points to the connection manager that we've created in the previous step, as shown in the following screenshot:

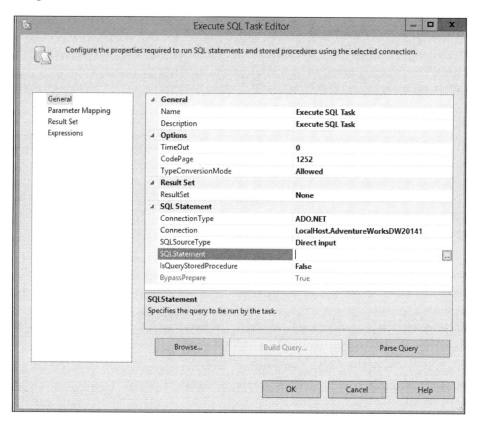

We now create a SQL statement for the incremental loading of the ProspectiveBuyer table. For the sake of simplicity, we will limit this example only to those columns that are directly mapped to the DimCustomer table.

We enter the statement in the **SQLStatement** section and get the following page:

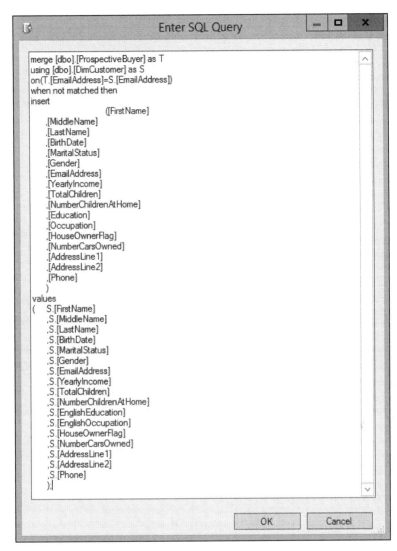

```
merge [dbo].[ProspectiveBuyer] as T
using [dbo].[DimCustomer] as S
on(T.[EmailAddress]=S.[EmailAddress])
when not matched then
insert
                        ([FirstName]
    ,[MiddleName]
    ,[LastName]
    ,[BirthDate]
    ,[MaritalStatus]
    ,[Gender]
    ,[EmailAddress]
    ,[YearlyIncome]
    ,[TotalChildren]
    ,[NumberChildrenAtHome]
    ,[Education]
    ,[Occupation]
    ,[HouseOwnerFlag]
    ,[NumberCarsOwned]
    ,[AddressLine1]
    ,[AddressLine2]
    ,[Phone]
    )
values
(    S.[FirstName]
    ,S.[MiddleName]
    ,S.[LastName]
    ,S.[BirthDate]
    ,S.[MaritalStatus]
    ,S.[Gender]
    ,S.[EmailAddress]
    ,S.[YearlyIncome]
    ,S.[TotalChildren]
    ,S.[NumberChildrenAtHome]
    ,S.[EnglishEducation]
    ,S.[EnglishOccupation]
    ,S.[HouseOwnerFlag]
    ,S.[NumberCarsOwned]
    ,S.[AddressLine1]
    ,S.[AddressLine2]
    ,S.[Phone]
    );
```

We click on **OK** and then close the Execute SQL Task Editor.

We now have a basic package ready, which will only insert the updated records in the `ProspectiveBuyer` table. We now deploy the project from the SQL Server to the Integration Services Catalog and then we can schedule this package to be executed at specific intervals, which we might need.

Summary

Ingesting data into your data warehouse and determining the dimensions and measures are the first steps towards building a data mining solution. In this chapter, you saw how we can use the SQL Server components such as Migration Assistant and Integration Services to integrate data from different sources. It is very likely that a business process will have multiple components for each department, and the source of data could be diverse. You will need to find a way to aggregate the required data from multiple sources such as flat files, Oracle, DB2, and so on, and then load it into your SQL Server database where you will perform the data mining operations. Finally, once such a data ingestion process is ready, you can schedule a data load periodically as per your need using the SQL Server Agent jobs. In the next chapter, we will dive into the algorithms that SQL Server provides for mining operations on the data. Knowing each of the algorithms in detail will help you pick the correct ones and implement them based on your specific need or criteria.

5
Classification Models

In the previous chapters, we saw how to use a data mining model to make predictions for a business problem that we framed in *Chapter 3, Tools of the Trade*. It is worthwhile to take a look at how each of these algorithms are framed, what are their properties, and how the output of these algorithms vary with a change in these properties. A common task in data mining can be categorizing a particular case (categories being one of the many possible outcomes of cases, and case being a group of records corresponding to a single entity). If we take the example of an employee, the categories could be service life, member of leadership team, salary, and so on, while the case would contain the data (attributes) of the current employees such as tenure, salary, employee ID, educational qualification, and so on. The data corresponding to a single employee will be a case, and the data corresponding to many employees will be a case set. We can use the case set to classify any further cases in some of the predefined categories using the classification models. Microsoft SQL Server Analysis Services Data Mining provides a query language, which can be used to define, modify, and query the models. It is commonly referred to as **Data Mining Extensions (DMX)**. In this chapter, we will work with some of the most commonly used classification models along with DMX that can be used for various operations on the models.

In this chapter, we will cover the following topics:

- Input, output, and predicted columns
- The feature selection
- The Microsoft Decision Tree algorithm and DMX
- The Microsoft Neural Network algorithm and DMX
- The Microsoft Naïve Bayes algorithm and DMX

Input, output, and predicted columns

You are familiar with the predictable columns from *Chapter 2, Data Model Preparation and Deployment*, but let's talk briefly about the input, output, and predicted columns in this chapter.

Input columns are the columns whose value is used as an input to the data mining model to predict an output. If a column is marked **Predict Only**, the columns are both predictable and output columns, but if a column is marked **Predict**, then the column is both an input and output column.

The feature selection

The feature selection requires a special notice because it helps in the selection of the attributes that will be effective in the analysis. It also helps in the rejection of the attributes that are either too noisy or are very insignificant in the analysis. Hence, the feature selection mostly involves the selection of appropriate attributes. A default feature selection is done automatically based on the model selected, the data types of the attributes, and the parameters (if any) that might be set up while designing the model. Every attribute that is designated to be a part of the model is assigned a score; the score threshold is also modifiable. The feature selection comprises of various methods that depends on whether the data is continuous or discrete. For continuous data, we use the interestingness score to select the columns that are more closely related, whereas for discrete methods, we use Shannon's entropy, Bayesian algorithm with K2 Prior, and the Bayesian algorithm with Uniform Prior. We will not go into the details of these preceding set of algorithms, but will understand the parameters that we can alter, which will modify the feature selection behavior of the algorithm and data model. The MSDN article at http://msdn.microsoft.com/en-us/library/ms175382.aspx gives more details about the feature selection process for different algorithms.

We will now see how we can alter the parameters to modify the feature selection methodology for any model. We will also use the Microsoft Decision Tree algorithm for our example. We already saw how we can create a data mining structure and add a data mining model to it. In *Chapter 2, Data Model Preparation and Deployment*, we looked at the **Mining Accuracy** tab, whereas in this chapter, we will work on the **Mining Models** tab, as shown in the following screenshot. We will choose **Age**, **Gender**, and **House Owner Flag** as the predictable columns because we want to understand the age, gender, and the house owner status of our customers and probably categorize the customers according to these three criteria. So, we can predict, for example, whether a particular combination of age, gender, and house owner will be our customers or not.

We will discuss the model and the attribute selection in the later part of this chapter. Let's look at how we can alter the feature selection in this section.

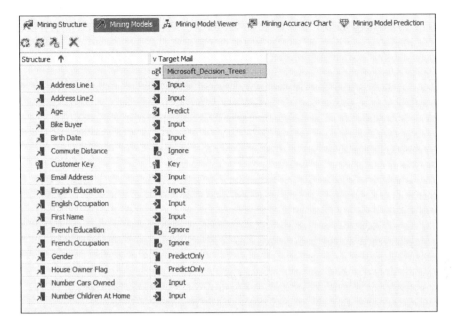

Click on the three circles next to **Set algorithm parameters** in the following **Properties** pane (which can be opened by right-clicking on the highlighted model in the preceding screenshot):

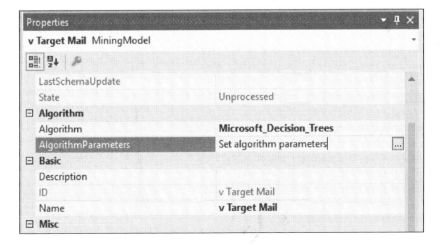

The following screen will open and help us modify the parameters for the feature selection:

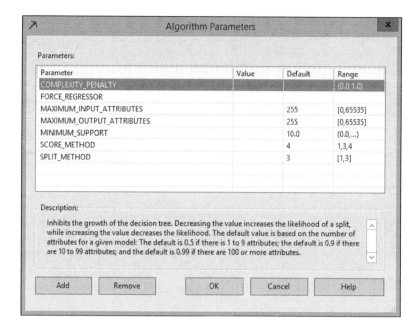

Let's now see what these parameters mean:

- `MAXIMUM_INPUT_ATTRIBUTES`: This parameter counts the number of columns and ignores any columns that are calculated as uninteresting (if the number of columns are more than this parameter)

- `MAXIMUM_OUTPUT_ATTRIBUTES`: This parameter counts the number of columns and ignores any columns that are calculated as uninteresting (if the number of predictable columns are more than this parameter)

We will discuss the methods, namely, `COMPLEXITY_PENALTY`, `FORCE_REGRESSOR`, `MINIMUM_SUPPORT`, `SCORE_METHOD`, and `SPLIT_METHOD` as and when we discuss the various data mining models.

The Microsoft Decision Tree algorithm

The Decision Tree algorithm is a classification and regression algorithm built for both discrete and continuous attribute predictions. The model works by building a tree with a number of splits or nodes. There is a new split or node added every time a column is found to be significantly related to the predictable columns.

The feature selection process, as explained in the previous section, is used to select the most useful attributes because the inclusion of too many attributes might cause a degradation of the performance during the processing of an algorithm and will eventually lead to low memory. When the performance is paramount, the following methods can:

- Increase the value of the COMPLEXITY_PENALTY parameter to limit the tree growth
- Limit the number of items in the association models to limit the number of trees built
- Increase the value of the MINIMUM_SUPPORT parameter to avoid overfitting
- Restrict the number of discrete values for any attribute to 10 or less

The problem of a data mining algorithm becoming overtrained or overfitted to a particular data set is common, and this often makes the model not usable for other data sets. Therefore, we can use certain parameters with the help of which we can control the growth or splitting of the tree. The MSDN article at http://msdn.microsoft. com/en-us/library/cc645868.aspx under the heading **Customizing the Decision Trees Algorithm** discusses the parameters that we can set to alter the model.

For a Microsoft Decision Tree algorithm, we require certain conditions to be met, as shown in the following screenshot:

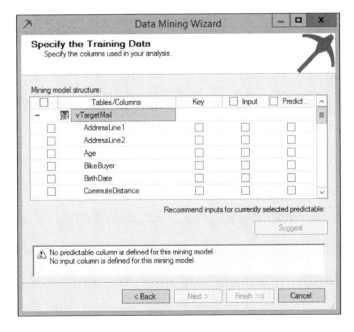

As evident from the preceding screenshot, we will require one **Key** column, at least one **Input** column, and at least one **Predictable** value. As we can see that the model has a tree as its foundation structure, we need to understand how the different attributes are selected to build a tree and why other attributes are neglected.

Let's take the example of the model where we are predicting **House Owner Flag**, as shown here:

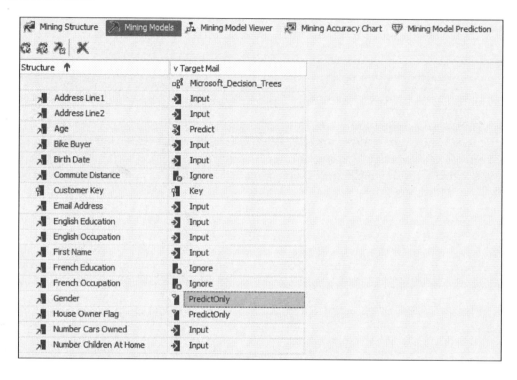

Under the **Mining Model Viewer** tab in the SQL Server Data Tools, the Decision Tree algorithm will appear, as shown in the following screenshot:

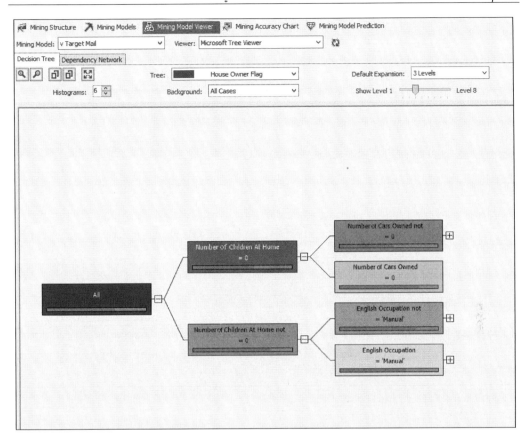

The tree is a representative of **House Owner Flag,** and we can see in the preceding screenshot whether a person is a house owner or not; he is very closely associated with the attribute indicating the number of children at home, which in turn has a very close relationship with the number of cars owned and English occupation. We can further drill down the tree to see more correlated attributes.

The parameter for the preceding Decision Tree model can be accessed using the methodology discussed in *The feature selection* in this chapter. Before we discuss the effect of altering various parameters, let's take a look at the parameters, as follows:

- COMPLEXITY_PENALTY: This controls the number of splits or growth of the Decision Tree algorithm and can also be used to optimize the processing efficiency as discussed previously in this chapter

- FORCE_REGRESSOR: This attribute uses certain columns irrespective of whether the columns are rated high on the feature selection score or not

- MAXIMUM_INPUT_ATTRIBUTES: These are the number of input attributes that the algorithm will safely consume before it invokes the feature selection

- MAXIMUM_OUTPUT_ATTRIBUTES: These are the number of output attributes that the algorithm can handle before it invokes the feature selection

- MINIMUM_SUPPORT: These are the minimum number of cases before the algorithm generates a split

- SCORE_METHOD: This is the algorithm that is used to determine the split score. More details can be found at http://msdn.microsoft.com/en-us/library/cc645868.aspx

- SPLIT_METHOD: This is the methodology for the split and is explained in detail in the MSDN article at http://msdn.microsoft.com/en-us/library/cc645868.aspx

Let's see the effect of changing the COMPLEXITY_PENALTY parameter in the Decision Tree algorithm. When the value of this parameter is set close to zero, there is a low penalty on the tree growth and you might see large trees. When its value is set close to one, the tree growth is penalized heavily and the resulting trees are relatively small. Generally speaking, large trees tend to have overtraining issues, whereas small trees might miss some patterns.

The recommended way to tune the model is to try multiple trees with different settings. Then, use cross validation to see where you get the highest and most stable accuracy.

The first few nodes split with the default `COMPLEXITY_PENALTY` value, as shown in the following screenshot:

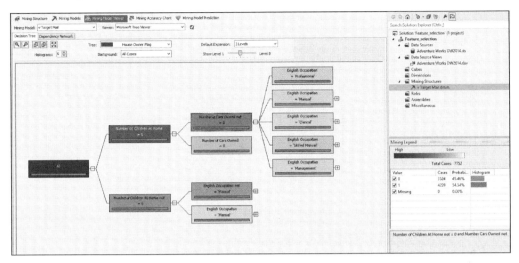

Decision Tree with the initial set of splits

We already discussed the lift charts and the associated information in *Chapter 2, Data Model Preparation and Deployment*. We will now use the concepts that we gained in *Chapter 2, Data Model Preparation and Deployment* to analyze the lift chart for the preceding model.

The data mining accuracy lift chart for the preceding model is shown in the following screenshot:

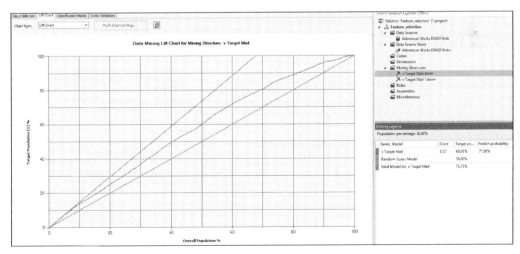

The Lift Chart for the preceding Decision Tree Model

We will now alter the value of COMPLEXITY_PENALTY to 0.99, as shown here:

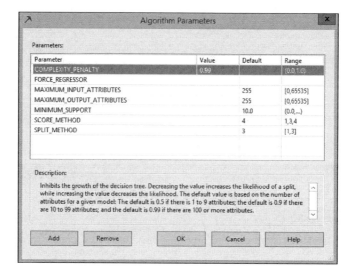

The tree split now has much fewer nodes, as shown here:

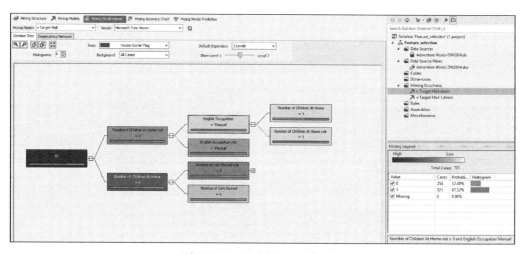

The Mining Model Viewer details

The lift chart for the preceding tree split is shown here:

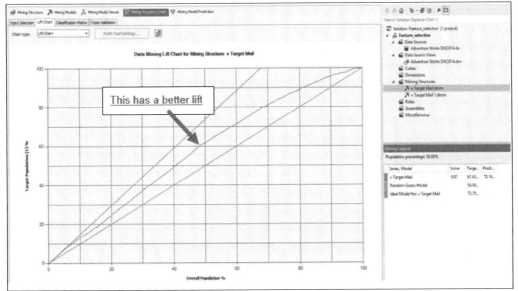

The lift chart after changing the parameters

This gives us an important observation. We can reduce the splits and still achieve the same lift; in fact, a better lift. Moreover, this saves a lot of processing time, and although this does not boost any performance under the current set of data, it is a boon for a large set of data and many attributes. It is to be noted here that although reducing the split has given us a better lift, it could also result in a worse lift. This is heavily dependent on the distribution of the attribute, as well as the information gained from the attribute. Lift might also vary with the data volume that is being used to train the model. As we can see, the dependency of the **House Owner Flag** attribute shifted from **Number of Children at home = 0** to **Number of Children at Home not 0**.

Let's now set the value of the MAXIMUM_INPUT_ATTRIBUTES parameter to 8, as shown in the following screenshot, the default value being 255:

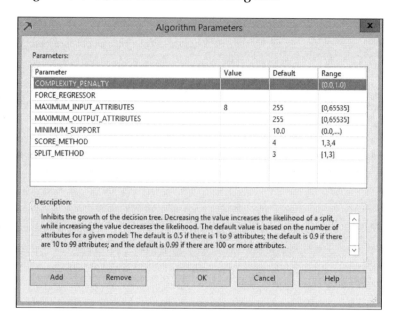

Let's look at the tree after setting up the parameter, as shown in the following screenshot. Notice how the tree splits and the correlation of the attributes vary.

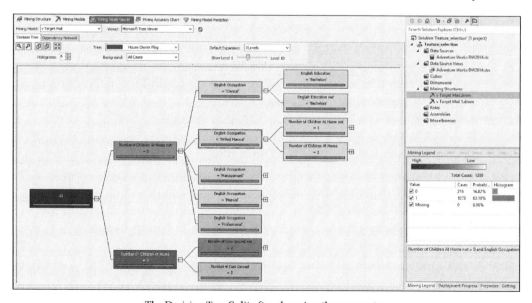

The Decision Tree Split after changing the parameter

Let's now alter the value of MAXIMUM_OUTPUT_PARAMETERS that has the value **255** as default.

The SCORE_METHOD parameter is used to calculate the split score as discussed in *The feature selection* earlier in this chapter. The values that are applicable for this parameter are shown
in the following table:

Value	Name
1	Entropy
3	Bayesian with K2 Prior
4	**Bayesian Dirichlet Equivalent (BDE)** with uniform prior

The MSDN article at http://msdn.microsoft.com/en-us/library/ms175382.aspx gives more details about these scoring methods.

We will change the value to 1. The resultant tree is shown here:

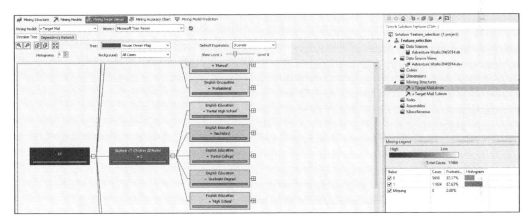

Decision Tree after changing the value of the SCORE_METHOD to 1

We can also see the lift chart, as shown in the following screenshot:

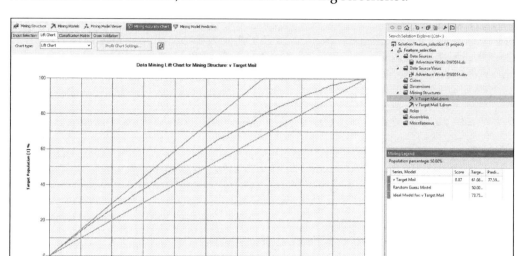

The lift chart after changing the value of the SCORE_METHOD to 1

Data Mining Extensions for the Decision Tree algorithm

Data Mining Extensions can be used to perform every activity that we have done from the user interface. We will not be looking at the queries to create the models, but will be looking at the examples of accessing various parameters of the data mining model. We will also look at how to frame a prediction query. The link `http://msdn.microsoft.com/en-us/library/hh230820.aspx` provides a complete list of **Dynamic Management Views (DMV)** for SSAS, although it refers to the 2012 version, it is equally valid for 2014. The link `http://technet.microsoft.com/en-us/library/ms132048.aspx` will give us the information about various pieces of data that we can extract from a data mining model. Also, the link `http://technet.microsoft.com/en-us/library/bb522459.aspx` will give us information about DMX on the whole.

Let's connect to the SQL Server Analysis Services using the SQL Server Management Studio, as shown in the following screenshot:

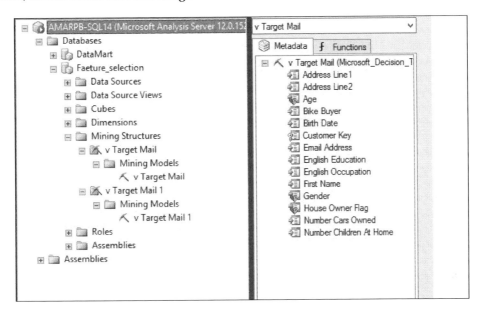

Let's query for `MINING_PARAMETERS` from the `v Target Mail` data mining using `DMSCHEMA_MINING_MODELS`, as shown in the following screenshot. The query executed is as follows:

```
Select MINING_PARAMETERS from $system.DMSCHEMA_MINING_MODELS where
MODEL_NAME='v Target Mail';
```

The result of the preceding query is shown in the following screenshot:

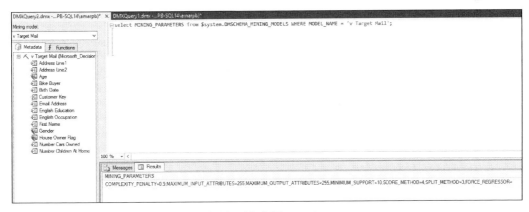

Mining Model Parameters

Let's now query the model for the name of the model, the name of the node and the children cardinality, and the statistics for the distribution of values in the node, as shown in the following screenshot. You can refer to `http://technet.microsoft.com/en-us/library/ms132064.aspx` for more details about the content of the model. The following query is executed:

```
Select MODEL_NAME, NODE_NAME, NODE_CAPTION,
NODE_SUPPORT, [CHILDREN_CARDINALITY], Node_distribution
FROM [v Target Mail].CONTENT
WHERE NODE_TYPE = 2
```

The result of the preceding query is shown in the following screenshot:

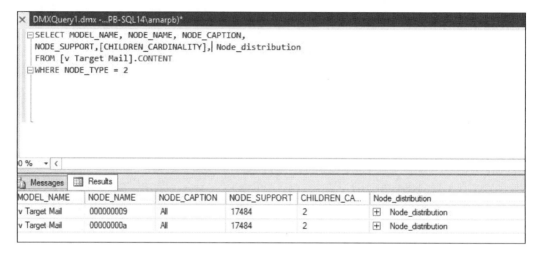

There might be instances where we have to write queries to predict certain values. Although, we can write the queries from the ground up, my personal favorite is to get the skeleton of the query from the query designer and make the appropriate changes. Let's navigate to the SQL Server Data Tools, as shown in the following screenshot:

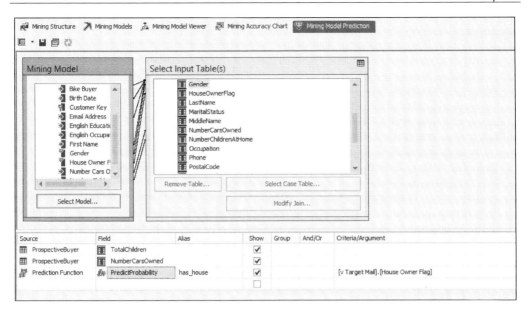

We now switch to the **Query** mode, as shown here:

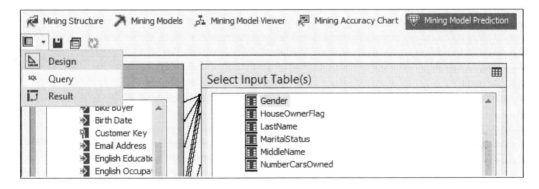

We will get the skeleton query, as shown in the following screenshot. The query that is executed is as follows:

```
SELECT
    t.[TotalChildren],
    t.[NumberCarsOwned],
    (PredictProbability([v Target Mail].[House Owner Flag])) as
[has_house]
From
    [v Target Mail]
PREDICTION JOIN
    OPENQUERY([Adventure Works DW2014],
'SELECT
    [TotalChildren],
    [NumberCarsOwned],
    [FirstName],
    [BirthDate],
    [Gender],
    [EmailAddress],
    [NumberChildrenAtHome],
    [HouseOwnerFlag],
    [AddressLine1],
    [AddressLine2]
FROM
    [dbo].[ProspectiveBuyer]
')AS t
ON
    [v Target Mail].[First Name] = t.[FirstName] AND
    [v Target Mail].[Birth Date] = t.[BirthDate] AND
    [v Target Mail].[Gender]=t.[Gender] AND
    [v Target Mail].[Email Address] = t.[EmailAddress] AND
    [v Target Mail].[Number Children At Home]=t.
    [ NumberChildrenAtHome] AND
    [v Target Mail].[House Owner Flag] = t.[HouseOwnerFlag] AND
    [v Target Mail].[Number Cars Owned] = t.[NumberCarsOwned] AND
    [v Target Mail].[Address Line1] = t.[AddressLine1] AND
    [v Target Mail].[ Address Line2] = t.[Address Line2]
```

Once you enter the preceding query, the interface will look like this:

```
SELECT
    t.[TotalChildren],
    t.[NumberCarsOwned],
    (PredictProbability([v Target Mail].[House Owner Flag])) as [has_house]
From
    [v Target Mail]
PREDICTION JOIN
    OPENQUERY([Adventure Works DW2014],
      'SELECT
        [TotalChildren],
        [NumberCarsOwned],
        [FirstName],
        [BirthDate],
        [Gender],
        [EmailAddress],
        [NumberChildrenAtHome],
        [HouseOwnerFlag],
        [AddressLine1],
        [AddressLine2]
      FROM
        [dbo].[ProspectiveBuyer]
      ') AS t
ON
    [v Target Mail].[First Name] = t.[FirstName] AND
    [v Target Mail].[Birth Date] = t.[BirthDate] AND
    [v Target Mail].[Gender] = t.[Gender] AND
    [v Target Mail].[Email Address] = t.[EmailAddress] AND
    [v Target Mail].[Number Children At Home] = t.[NumberChildrenAtHome] AND
    [v Target Mail].[House Owner Flag] = t.[HouseOwnerFlag] AND
    [v Target Mail].[Number Cars Owned] = t.[NumberCarsOwned] AND
    [v Target Mail].[Address Line1] = t.[AddressLine1] AND
    [v Target Mail].[Address Line2] = t.[AddressLine2]
```

We will now execute the preceding query against the deployed model, as seen here:

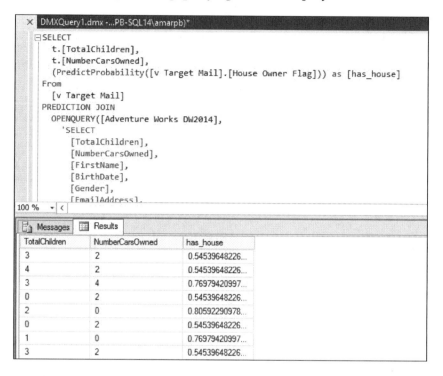

Now that the query is ready, we can apply any filtration that we want and get the appropriate results. We can follow the same method to get the query for any of the functions, as seen in the following screenshot:

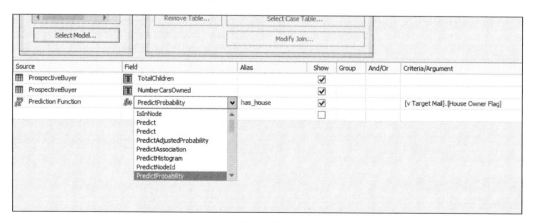

Applying filtration

The Microsoft Neural Network algorithm

The Microsoft Neural Network algorithm uses a combination of each state of the input variable and each state of the output variable to form a series of networks or neurons. It uses the input to calculate the probabilities for a particular outcome. The complex structure of the algorithm lends its usefulness for complex analysis, such as stock movement, currency fluctuation, and so on. The Microsoft Neural Network algorithm is based on a multilayer perceptron network, which consists of multiple layers, namely the input layer, hidden layer (which is optional), and output layer. We will look at the parameters for the algorithm and also how their alteration affects the output of the predictable values later in this chapter. The three layers of the model are briefly described as follows:

- **Input layer**: This layer defines all the input attribute values for the data mining model
- **Hidden layer**: The probabilities of the input values are the assigned weights in this layer; the weight resembles the favoring of the result with a particular input attribute
- **Output layer**: This layer represents the predictable attribute values

The MSDN article at `http://msdn.microsoft.com/en-us/library/ms174941.aspx` and `http://msdn.microsoft.com/en-us/library/cc645901.aspx` gives further explanation of the concepts related to the Microsoft Neural Network algorithm.

We will now design the data mining model using the Microsoft Neural Network algorithm with the **Input**, **Key**, and **Output** columns, as shown in the following screenshot:

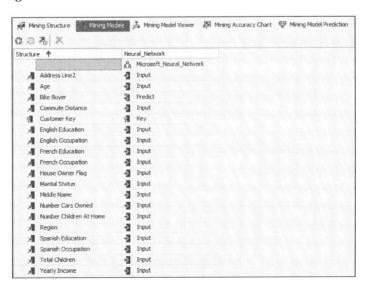

The **Mining Model Viewer** tab gives us the following view of the model:

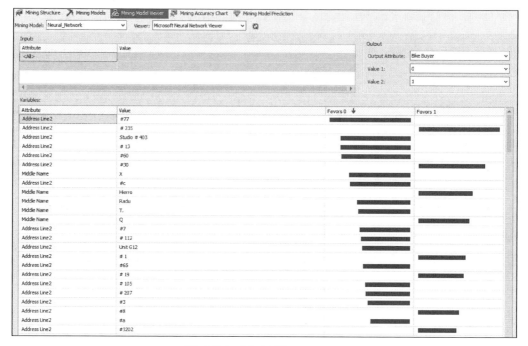

The Mining Model Viewer screen

We will now discuss each section in the preceding screenshot, namely, the **Input**, **Output**, and **Variables** sections.

The **Input** section gives us the ability to choose the input whose value will be used to serve as an input for the model. By default, we are looking at all the attributes as the input with their certain default values. The **Output** section gives us information about the attribute for which we seek information. In this case, the attribute whose behavior we seek to examine is **Bike Buyer**. The **Variables** section gives us information about the favors a particular attribute has towards any of the values of the output attribute. For example, considering all the input attributes, we can see in the preceding screenshot that the people with **Address Line2** as **#235** have more likelihood of buying a bike.

We will now discuss the parameters of the algorithm and the effect of changing their values on the algorithm behavior. The following screenshot shows the parameters for the algorithm and the method to access these parameters will remain the same for every model irrespective of the algorithm:

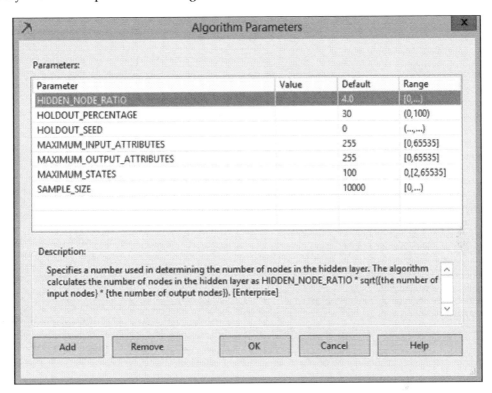

The parameters that control the feature selection of the algorithm are MAXIMUM_INPUT_ATTRIBUTES, MAXIMUM_OUTPUT_ATTRIBUTES, and MAXIMUM_STATES. Let's look at how varying each parameter affects the outcome of the Microsoft Neural Network algorithm. The **Input** and **Predict** columns are shown in the following screenshot. Please note that although we have included several columns in the model, the users are encouraged to alter the input so that there is a better correlation between the input and the predictable attribute. An obvious example in the following screenshot is the inclusion of **French Education** and **French Occupation**.

These can be removed from the selection as they have a 1:1 correlation with **English Education** and **English Occupation**; therefore, their inclusion does not add any columns to the new inputs of the algorithm.

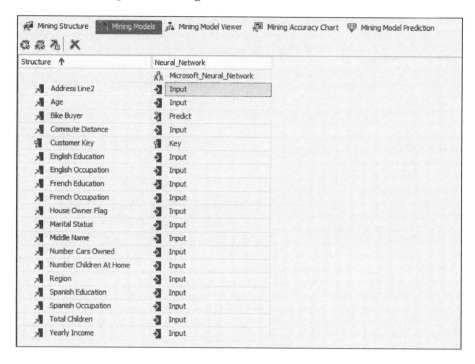

The lift chart for the preceding inputs is shown here:

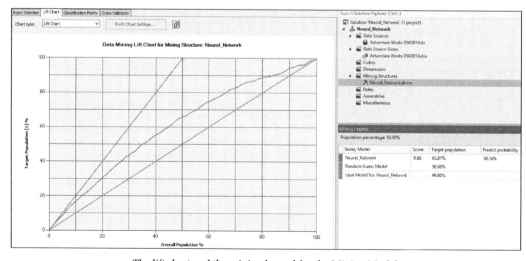

The lift chart and the mining legend for the Mining Model

As discussed in the previous model, `MAXIMUM_INPUT_ATTRIBUTES` lays down a limit on the number of input attributes before it starts to apply the feature selection. We will set this parameter to `10`, see the following lift chart:

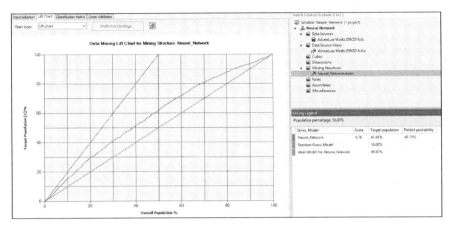

The lift chart with the MAXIMUM_INPUT_ATTRIBUTES to 10

In the preceding graph, we can see that there is a drop in **Score**, **Target population**, and **Predict probability**. This clearly is an indication that there is an opportunity to refine the input models so that a better score and probability can be achieved.

We also know that `MAXIMUM_OUTPUT_PARAMETERS` is the maximum number of output columns that can be assigned before the algorithm applies the feature selection. Let's set this parameter to `1`. As we already have only one predictable column, we won't see any change in the lift chart.

The `MAXIMUM_STATES` parameter imposes a limit on the number of discrete values or states that an attribute can have. We set the `MAXIMUM_STATES` parameter to `2` and view the model in the **Mining Model Viewer** tab, as shown in the following screenshot:

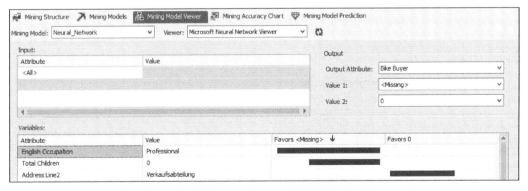

The Mining Model Viewer with the MAXIMUM_STATES set to 2

The value of **Value 1** in the **Output** attribute is worth noticing here. This clearly explains the importance of this parameter. If the value of this attribute is less than the number of the possible values of the **Output** attribute, it will only show the most popular attribute and display the value of remaining values as <Missing>.

The HIDDEN_NODE_RATIO parameter is the total number of hidden nodes to start with; the formula governing the number of hidden nodes is as follows:

```
HIDDEN_NODE_RATIO * SQRT(Total input neurons * Total output
neurons)
```

The Microsoft Generic Content Tree Viewer for the algorithm is shown in the following screenshot:

As we can see in the preceding screenshot, the node highlighted is the input layer and has the cardinality of **207**. Highlighting the node **(50000000000000000)**, we get the cardinality of **2**. Now, let's apply the following formula and calculate the value of the hidden layer:

Hidden layer = 4*floor (sqrt(207*2)) = 4*20 (taking the floor value) = 80

This is exactly the value that we see in the Microsoft Generic Content Tree Viewer. However, we know that the hidden layer is optional, so let's change this ratio to 0. The corresponding changes in the different layers are seen in the following screenshot:

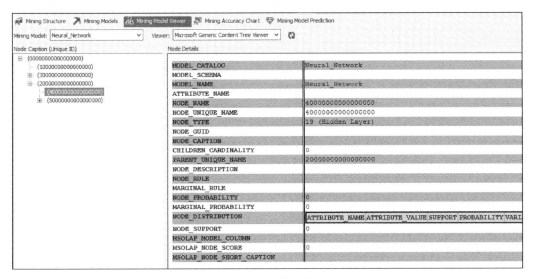

Generic Content Tree Viewer

The lift chart for the model with the changed value of the hidden layer is shown in the following screenshot:

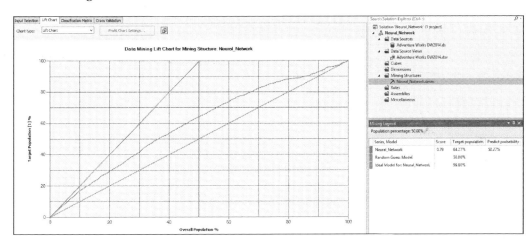

Lift chart with the value of CHILDREN_CARDINALITY set to zero

The lift chart for the model with `HIDDEN_NODE_RATIO = 10` is shown in the following screenshot:

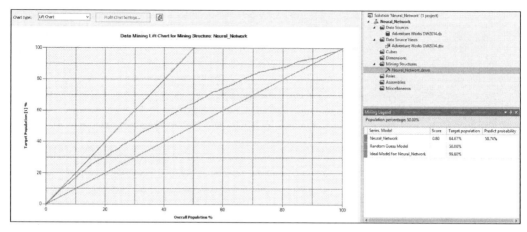

Lift chart with value of HIDDEN_NODE_RATIO equal to 10

In the preceding screenshot, we can observe that there is no change in the lift chart with a higher ratio. We will discuss the other parameters when we look at tuning the models for optimum results. For every attribute, we have the options for **ModelingFlags**, as shown in the following screenshot:

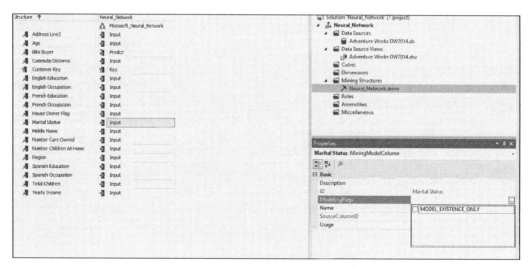

Setting the modeling flags for Neural_Network model

These values suggest that the actual value of the attribute is of little importance, what really matters is whether the attribute has a value or not.

Data Mining Extensions for the Neural Network algorithm

We will now try to perform the administrative steps that we performed with the help of a user interface using DMX. The link `http://technet.microsoft.com/en-us/library/cc645876.aspx` provides more detail about the data mining model. Once we deploy the model to Analysis Services, we can get the metadata of the model. The query that is executed is as follows:

```
SELECT MODEL_NAME, DATE_CREATED, LAST_PROCESSED,
PREDICTION_ENTITY, MINING_PARAMETERS
from $system.DMSCHEMA_MINING_MODELS
WHERE MODEL_NAME='Neural_Network'
```

The result of the preceding query is shown in the following screenshot:

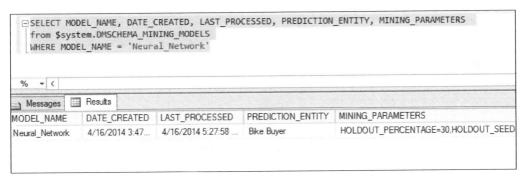

The query that will be used to get the values of the input layer, the hidden layer, and the output layer is as follows:

```
Select model_name,Node_name,node_type,[children_cardinality],
node_distribution from [Neural_Network].CONTENT where node_type=18
or node_type=19 or node_type=20;
```

The output of the preceding query is shown in the following screenshot:

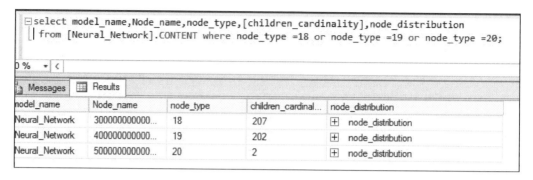

Now, let's get the names of the nodes that are present in the hidden layer. The query that is executed is as follows:

```
Select model_name,Node_name,node_type,node_distribution
from [Neural_Network].CONTENT where node_type = 22;
```

The result of the preceding query is shown in the following screenshot:

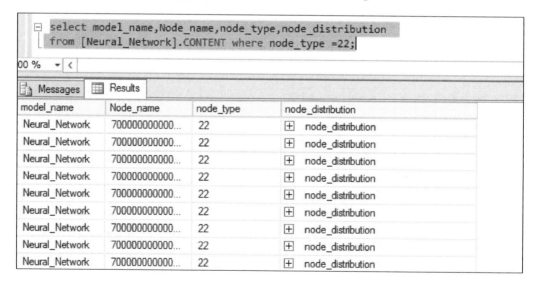

The details of a particular node in the hidden layer are shown in the next screenshot; the query that is executed is as follows:

```
SELECT FLATTENED TOP 1 NODE_UNIQUE_NAME,
(SELECT ATTRIBUTE_NAME,ATTRIBUTE_VALUE,VALUETYPE
FROM NODE_DISTRIBUTION) as t
```

```
FROM [Neural_Network].CONTENT
WHERE NODE_TYPE = 22
AND [PARENT_UNIQUE_NAME] = '40000000000000000'
```

The result of the preceding query is shown in the following screenshot:

```
SELECT FLATTENED TOP 1 NODE_UNIQUE_NAME,
(SELECT ATTRIBUTE_NAME, ATTRIBUTE_VALUE, VALUETYPE
FROM NODE_DISTRIBUTION) as t
FROM  [Neural_Network].CONTENT
WHERE NODE_TYPE = 22
AND [PARENT_UNIQUE_NAME] = '40000000000000000'
```

NODE_UNIQUE_NAME	t.ATTRIBUTE_NAME	t.ATTRIBUTE_VALUE	t.VALUETYPE
70000000000000000	6000000000000005d	-0.0547081334346669	7
70000000000000000	6000000000000005e	0.0968067412589735	7
70000000000000000	6000000000000005f	0.0561043599171	7
70000000000000000	60000000000000060	0.101136825476671	7
70000000000000000	60000000000000061	0.110710231862266	7
70000000000000000	60000000000000062	0.0210718610392634	7
70000000000000000	60000000000000063	-0.0077985160132568	7
70000000000000000	60000000000000064	0.0255755548256862	7
70000000000000000	60000000000000067	0.0607794514415159	7
70000000000000000	60000000000000068	-0.103709924285029	7
70000000000000000	60000000000000069	0.00137172372255841	7
70000000000000000	6000000000000006a	0.0695686503196296	7
70000000000000000	6000000000000006b	-0.0505411072799909	7
70000000000000000	6000000000000006c	-0.00159906735342293	7

We will now try to frame a prediction query using SSDT as we have done in the previous model, as shown here:

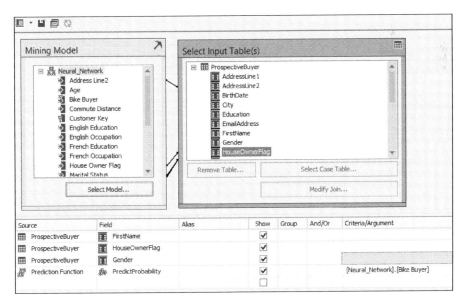

The following screenshot shows the other prediction function that is available to frame the prediction queries for a **Neural Network** model:

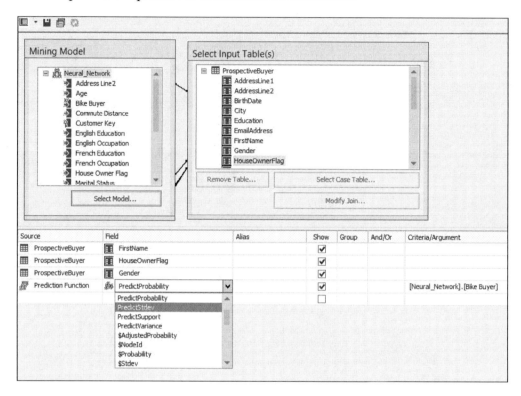

The prediction query that was framed is shown in the next screenshot. The query is as follows:

```
SELECT
    t.[FirstName],
    t.[HouseOwnerFlag],
    t.[Gender]
    (PredictProbability([Neural_Network].[Bike Buyer]))
From
    [Neural_Network]
PREDICTION JOIN
    OPENQUERY([Adventure Works DW2014],
        'SELECT
            [FirstName],
            [HouseOwnerFlag],
            [Gender],
            [MiddleName],
            [MaritalStatus],
```

```
            [YearlyIncome],
            [TotalChildren],
            [NumberChildrenAtHome],
            [NumberCarsOwned],
            [AddressLine2]
    FROM
            [dbo].[ProspectiveBuyer]
    ')AS t
ON
    [Neural_Network].[Middle Name] = t.[MiddleName] AND
    [Neural_Network].[Marital Status] = t.[MaritalStatus] AND
    [Neural_Network].[Yearly Income] = t.[YearlyIncome] AND
    [Neural_Network].[Total Children] = t.[TotalChildren] AND
    [Neural_Network].[Number Children At Home] = t.[
      NumberChildrenAtHome] AND
    [Neural_Network].[House Owner Flag] = t.[HouseOwnerFlag] AND
    [Neural_Network].[Number Cars Owned] = t.[NumberCarsOwned] AND
    [Neural_Network].[Address Line2] = t.[Address Line2]
```

Once you enter the preceding query, the interface will look like this:

```
SELECT
    t.[FirstName],
    t.[HouseOwnerFlag],
    t.[Gender],
    PredictProbability([Neural_Network].[Bike Buyer])
From
    [Neural_Network]
PREDICTION JOIN
    OPENQUERY([Adventure Works DW2014],
        'SELECT
            [FirstName],
            [HouseOwnerFlag],
            [Gender],
            [MiddleName],
            [MaritalStatus],
            [YearlyIncome],
            [TotalChildren],
            [NumberChildrenAtHome],
            [NumberCarsOwned],
            [AddressLine2]
        FROM
            [dbo].[ProspectiveBuyer]
        ') AS t
ON
    [Neural_Network].[Middle Name] = t.[MiddleName] AND
    [Neural_Network].[Marital Status] = t.[MaritalStatus] AND
    [Neural_Network].[Yearly Income] = t.[YearlyIncome] AND
    [Neural_Network].[Total Children] = t.[TotalChildren] AND
    [Neural_Network].[Number Children At Home] = t.[NumberChildrenAtHome] AND
    [Neural_Network].[House Owner Flag] = t.[HouseOwnerFlag] AND
    [Neural_Network].[Number Cars Owned] = t.[NumberCarsOwned] AND
    [Neural_Network].[Address Line2] = t.[AddressLine2]
```

We can execute this query by customizing or executing it as it is.

The Microsoft Naïve Bayes algorithm

Imagine a newborn witnessing his first sunset. Being new to this world, he doesn't know whether the sun will rise again. Making a guess, he gives the chance of a sunrise even odds and places a black marble in a bag that represents no sunrise and a white marble that represents a sunrise. As each day passes, the child places in the bag a marble based on the evidence he witnesses—in this case, a white marble for each sunrise. Over time, the black marble becomes lost in a sea of white, and the child can say with near certainty that the sun will rise each day.

This was the example posed by Reverend Thomas Bayes in his 1763 paper establishing the methodology that is now one of the fundamental principles of modern Machine Learning. This is the foundation of the Microsoft Naïve Bayes algorithm. This is one of the least resource-intensive algorithms and is often used for the initial analysis of data so that we get an idea about the trends presented in the data. Also, since we are not looking for any prediction, rather the distribution of data, we might as well keep the input data to the utmost required data by controlling the parameters: MINIMUM_INPUT_PARAMETERS, MINIMUM_OUTPUT_PARAMETERS, and MINIMUM_STATES. The MSDN article at http://msdn.microsoft.com/en-us/library/ms174806.aspx and http://msdn.microsoft.com/en-us/library/cc645902.aspx can be used to get more insights about how the algorithm governing the data mining model functions. As evident from the following screenshot, we will define at least one key column, one input column, and one predictable column to prepare a data mining model based on the Naïve Bayes Algorithm:

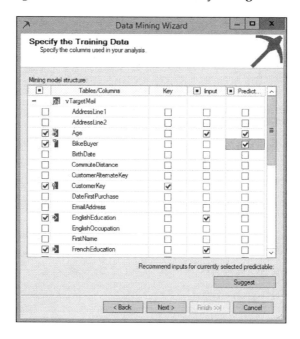

The structure of the data mining model in accordance with the input provided is shown in the following screenshot:

This is important as the Naïve Bayes algorithm cannot use columns with continuous values. Therefore, the values have to be discretized in order to allow the algorithms to find interesting patterns in the data. Discretization is the method of grouping the values into several buckets so that there are finite numbers of possible states of an attribute. The default number of discretization count is 5. The discretization method is another parameter that decides the method of discretization to be used. There are three main methods for discretization: `Automatic`, `Clusters`, and `Equal_Areas`. A brief discussion of these methods is as follows.

In the `Automatic` discretization method, Analysis Services chooses the method to group the value automatically. The `Clusters` method can only be used for numeric columns; however, it is more resource intensive, and this method works on any random distribution that involves segregating the data into random segments followed by running the **Expectation Maximization Clustering** method several times on these segments. The document `http://ai.stanford.edu/~chuongdo/papers/em_tutorial.pdf` has further information about the Expectation Maximization Clustering method.

The `Equal_Areas` method works on the principle of dividing the entire set of values into multiple groups. This method works best when the distribution is equal for the values and where an unequal distribution will produce inaccurate results. We will now see how it affects the model by varying these parameters that we created.

The discretization of an attribute can be verified by observing the content, as shown in the following screenshot:

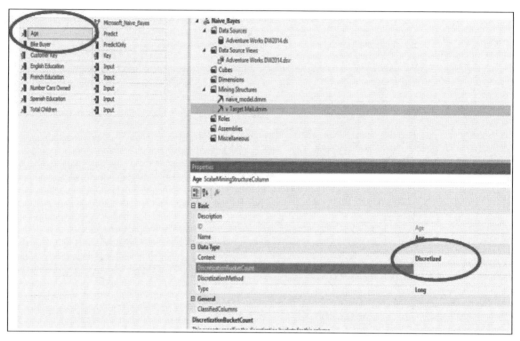

The variable age is Discretized

There are no values specified for the `DiscretizationBucketCount` and `DiscretizationMethod` properties, which means that the default values are being applied. We will now change the `DiscretizationBucketCount` property to 6, as shown here:

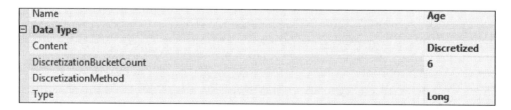

Name	Age
⊟ **Data Type**	
Content	**Discretized**
DiscretizationBucketCount	6
DiscretizationMethod	
Type	Long

The **Attribute profiles** tab in the Naïve Bayes viewer will appear, as shown in the following screenshot:

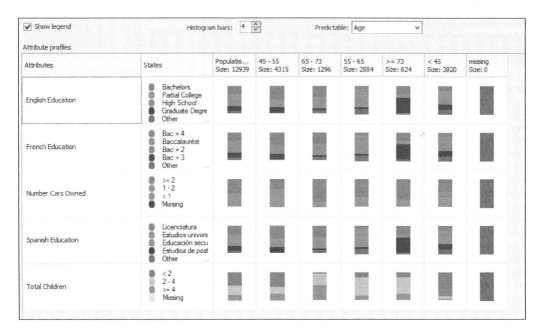

As we can see, there are six ranges in the age attribute that are listed against each of the input attribute. We will now change the ranges of values of total children and also change the discretization method, as shown in the following screenshot, and see its effect on the model. The `DiscretizationBucketCount` property is set to 4 and `DiscretizationMethod` is set to `Clusters`.

As we can see, the number of buckets for **Total Children** has reduced to **4** versus the previous **5** value. We will now change the discretization method to `Equal_Areas`; the resultant model can be seen in the following screenshot:

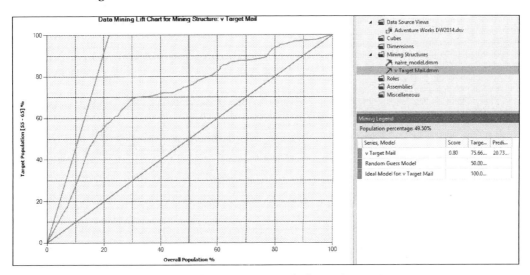

The question that is obvious now is which method should be chosen?
The lift chart with the discretization method is set to `Automatic`, as shown in the following screenshot:

Lift chart with Discretization method set to Automatic

The lift chart using `Clusters` as the method is shown in the following screenshot:

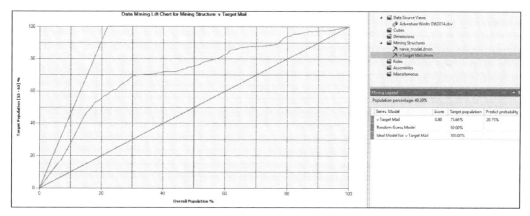

Lift chart using the "Clusters" as the Discretization method

The lift chart using `Equal_Areas` as the discretization method is shown in the following screenshot:

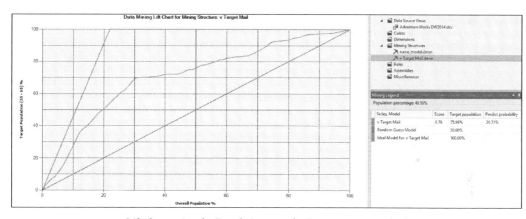

Lift chart using the Equal_Areas as the Discretization method

Thus, we can see that the score for the `Automatic` and `Cluster` methods are more or less the same, whereas the score for `Equal_Areas` is lower, so it would be preferable to go with the automatic bucketing method or clusters bucketing method for this attribute.

Data Mining Extensions for the Naïve Bayes algorithm

We will now be looking at DMX for the Naïve Bayes model. More details can be found at `http://technet.microsoft.com/en-us/library/cc645907.aspx`, and we will start by looking at `$system.DMSCHEMA_MINING_MODELS`, as shown in the next screenshot. The query that is executed is as follows:

```
Select model_name, prediction_entity,mining_parameters,training_set_
size
from $system.DMSCHEMA_MINING_MODELS where model_name='v Target Mail'
```

The result for the preceding query is as follows:

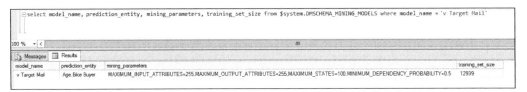

The Results tab

If we look at Generic Content Tree Viewer in the SSDT, we can see the following information for the attributes:

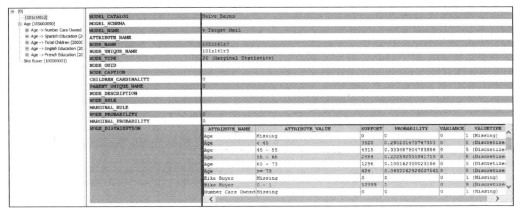

The Generic Content Tree Viewer attributes

The same information can be obtained with the help of the DMX query against the model. The query is as follows:

```
SELECT FLATTENED MODEL_NAME,
(SELECT ATTRIBUTE_NAME, ATTRIBUTE_VALUE, [SUPPORT], [PROBABILITY],
VALUETYPE FROM NODE_DISTRIBUTION) AS t
FROM [v Target Mail].CONTENT
WHERE NODE_TYPE = 26;
```

The result of the preceding query is shown in the following screenshot:

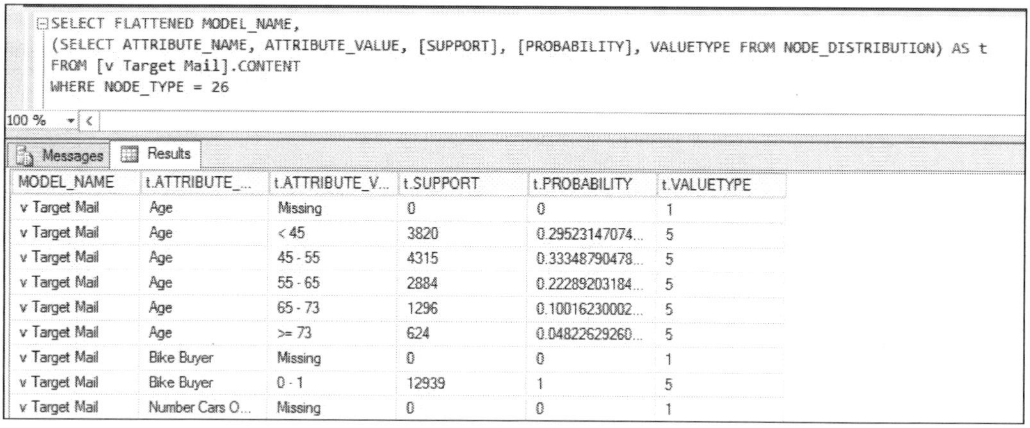

We will now try to make a few predictions using the model, as shown in the following screenshot. We will be forming a query that will predict the age of the buyer given the **City**, **EmailAddress**, **Gender**, **YearlyIncome**, and **HouseOwnerFlag**.

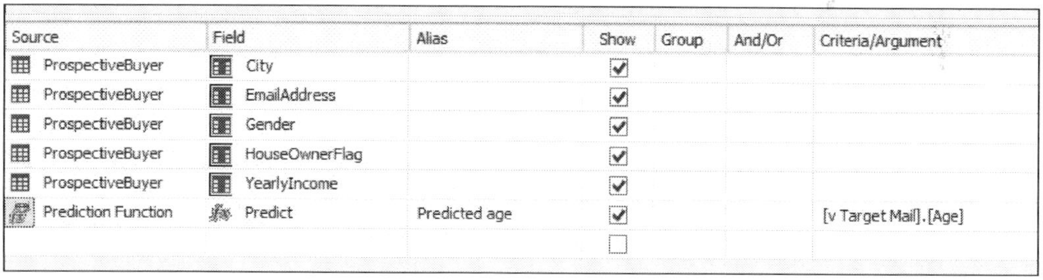

The result of the query is as follows:

City	EmailAddress	Gender	HouseOwnerFlag	YearlyIncome	Predicted age
Cedar City	aalexander@lu...	M	1	40000	60
Colma	aalonso@alpin...	F	1	80000	60
Lynnwood	aalvarez@fine...	M	1	130000	60
Chula Vista	aarun@advent...	M	1	50000	39
Dallas	abailey@lucern...	F	1	10000	50
Puyallup	abell@thephon...	M	0	50000	39
Colma	abennett@alpi...	F	1	50000	39
Culver City	abennett@cpa...	F	1	40000	60
Beverly Hills	abhat@adatum...	M	1	90000	39
Port Orchard	abrown@treyr...	F	0	40000	60
Edmonds	abryant@north...	F	1	60000	39
Puyallup	abryant@treyr...	F	1	40000	39
Pleasanton	abutler@cohov...	F	1	30000	39
West Covina	acarter@conto...	F	1	50000	39
Bellingham	acarter@margi...	M	1	70000	60
Citrus Heights	acastro@alpine...	F	1	50000	60
Spokane	acastro@theph...	M	1	30000	39
Berkeley	achande@adat...	F	0	50000	60
Los Angeles	achande@coho...	F	1	30000	50
Los Angeles	achander@coh...	M	1	30000	39
Dallas	achander@luce...	F	1	10000	60
Burien	achander@mar...	F	1	70000	60
Milwaukie	aclark@humon...	M	0	90000	60

The following **Query** pane will give us the result:

```
SELECT
  t.[City],
  t.[EmailAddress],
  t.[Gender],
  t.[HouseOwnerFlag],
  t.[YearlyIncome],
  (Predict ([v Target Mail].[Age])) as [Predicted age]
From
  [v Target Mail]
PREDICTION JOIN
  OPENQUERY([Adventure Works DW2014],
    'SELECT
      [City],
      [EmailAddress],
      [Gender],
      [HouseOwnerFlag],
      [YearlyIncome],
      [TotalChildren],
      [NumberCarsOwned]
    FROM
      [dbo].[ProspectiveBuyer]
    ') AS t
ON
  [v Target Mail].[Total Children] = t.[TotalChildren] AND
  [v Target Mail].[Number Cars Owned] = t.[NumberCarsOwned]
```

The probability functions that are available for the Naïve Bayes algorithm are as follows:

Now, let's try to predict the age of the individuals who own a house and are males. The query that we have is as follows:

```
SELECT
    t.[City],
    t.[EmailAddress],
    t.[Gender],
    t.[HouseOwnerFlag],
    t.[YearlyIncome],
    (Predict ([v Target Mail].[Age])) as [Predicted age]
From
    [v Target Mail]
PREDICTION JOIN
    OPENQUERY([Adventure Works DW2014],
      'SELECT
        [City],
        [EmailAddress],
        [Gender],
        [HouseOwnerFlag],
        [YearlyIncome],
        [TotalChildren],
        [NumberCarsOwned]
      FROM
        [dbo].[ProspectiveBuyer]
      ') AS t
ON
    [v Target Mail].[Total Children] = t.[TotalChildren] AND
    [v Target Mail].[Number Cars Owned] = t.[NumberCarsOwned]
```

All we have to do is add the where clause in the preceding query, as shown in the following query:

```
SELECT
  t.[City],
  t.[EmailAddress],
  t.[Gender],
  t.[HouseOwnerFlag],
  t.[YearlyIncome],
  (Predict ([v Target Mail].[Age])) as [Predicted age]
From
  [v Target Mail]
PREDICTION JOIN
  OPENQUERY([Adventure Works DW2014],
    'SELECT
      [City],
      [EmailAddress],
      [Gender],
      [HouseOwnerFlag],
      [YearlyIncome],
      [TotalChildren],
      [NumberCarsOwned]
    FROM
      [dbo].[ProspectiveBuyer]
    ') AS t
ON
  [v Target Mail].[Total Children] = t.[TotalChildren] AND
  [v Target Mail].[Number Cars Owned] = t.[NumberCarsOwned]
where t.[Gender]='M' and t.[HouseOwnerFlag]=1;
```

The result of the preceding query is shown in the following screenshot:

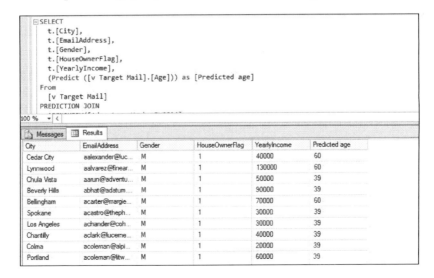

Summary

This chapter dealt with a few classification algorithms that are provided by the Microsoft SQL Server Analysis Services Data Mining suite. We walked through the examples using the Decision Tree algorithm, the Neural Network algorithm, and the Naïve Bayes algorithm and used DMX to change a few of their properties and frame prediction queries. Since this chapter was complex, it will be worthwhile for you to take a look at the links provided throughout the chapter. The next chapter will focus on the segmentation and association models in greater detail.

6
Segmentation and Association Models

In the previous chapter, you had an extensive look at the classification models. There are business requirements wherein the answer is not yes/no, but rather finding a relationship between the entities. A common example of this can be looking for similarity in the employees with a particular tenure in an organization or products bought by a section of society. The Microsoft Clustering algorithm helps us group the entities with the same attributes and study their common behavior, be it determining the buying patterns of one section of society or the investing patterns of a different one. The Microsoft Association algorithm helps us determine the placement of the products in a supermarket or helps suggest some additional products to the customer based on their purchase. We will alter their parameters to see the change in their behavior. At the end of this chapter, you will be able to use these algorithms to solve a business problem targeted towards determining groups of entities with common attributes, or build recommendation engines for the customer queries on their buying history and similar activities.

In this chapter, the following topics will be covered:

- The Microsoft Clustering algorithm
- Data Mining Extensions for the Microsoft Clustering algorithm
- The Microsoft Association algorithm
- Data Mining Extensions for the Microsoft Association algorithm

The Microsoft Clustering algorithm

The data mining models based on the Microsoft Clustering algorithm is targeted towards identifying the relationships between different entities of the dataset and dividing them into logically related groups. This algorithm differs from other algorithms in such a way that these do not require any predictable columns as their prime motive is to identify the groups of data, rather than to predict the value of an attribute. These groupings can then be used to make predictions, identify exceptions, and so on. Thus, the prime usage of this algorithm lies mainly in the data analysis phase where the focus is mainly on the existing/current data to test our hypothesis about the relationships between entities in the data and determine any exceptions (hidden relationships).

The following screenshot shows a data mining model based on the Microsoft Clustering algorithm. This can be seen in the **SSDT Mining Models** tab.

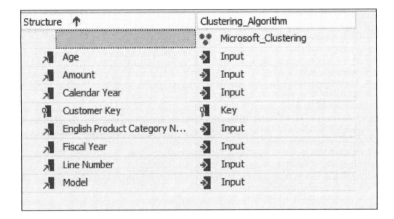

An important observation regarding the preceding screenshot is that we have not designated any column as a predictable column. This is okay since the Microsoft Clustering algorithm is mainly used in scenarios where we need to understand the segment of population and how differently this segment is correlated.

In the **Mining Model Viewer** tab of **SQL Server Data Tools** (**SSDT**), you can see the clustering model, as shown here:

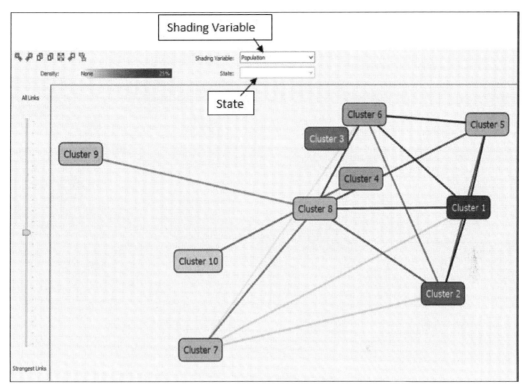

Mining Model Viewer for Clustering Model

The preceding graph shows the clusters that exist in the data mining model, which essentially is the grouping of the entities that have the similar characteristics, and the lines between these clusters shows the similarity between any two clusters. The shading of the two connected clusters is controlled by the shading variable and the state.

We now alter the **Shading Variable** field to **Age** and **State** to **Average (46-50)**, as shown in the following screenshot:

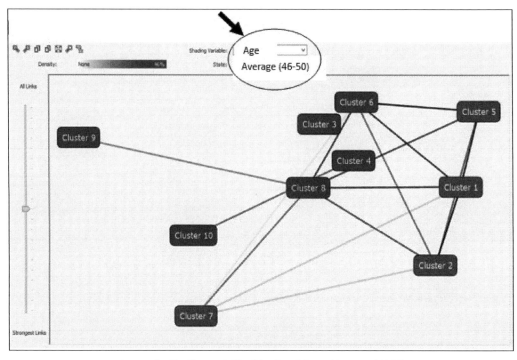

clusters for Shading variable="Age" and State="Average(46-50)"

We can immediately see that **Cluster 2** is very similar to **Cluster 1** and **Cluster 8** and so on. Also, the intensity of darkness of every cluster gives an idea about the population density of the shading variable and the state in that cluster.

We will now take a closer look at the clusters by navigating to the **Cluster Profiles** tab, as shown in the following screenshot:

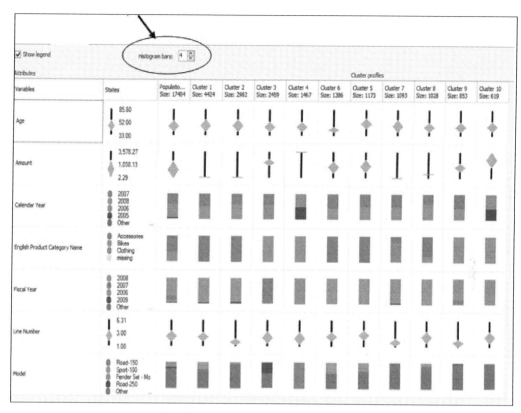

The Clusters with Histogram Bars equal to 4

The histogram bar variable controls the number of bars that are visible in the histogram for each attribute. If the number of histogram bars is more than the number specified, the bar of highest importance is displayed, while the other bars are grouped under a grey histogram. We can also infer that the concentration of the **Age** group in the first cluster is between **52** plus/minus some value. Now, the graph in the following screenshot shows that **Cluster 1** and **Cluster 2** are very similar when we look at the **Age** group of 46 to 58. A closer look at the two clusters shows similarity in most of the attributes, as shown here:

Variables	States		Cluster 1 Size: 4424	Cluster 2 Size: 2982
Age	85.80 52.00 33.00			
Amount	3,578.27 1,038.13 2.29			
Calendar Year		2007 2008 2006 2005 Other		
English Product Category Name		Accessories Bikes Clothing missing		
Fiscal Year		2008 2007 2006 2009 Other		
Line Number	6.31 3.00 1.00			
Model		Road-150 Sport-100 Fender Set - Mountain Road-250 Other		

We will now navigate to the **Cluster Characteristics** tab in SSDT, as shown in the following screenshot:

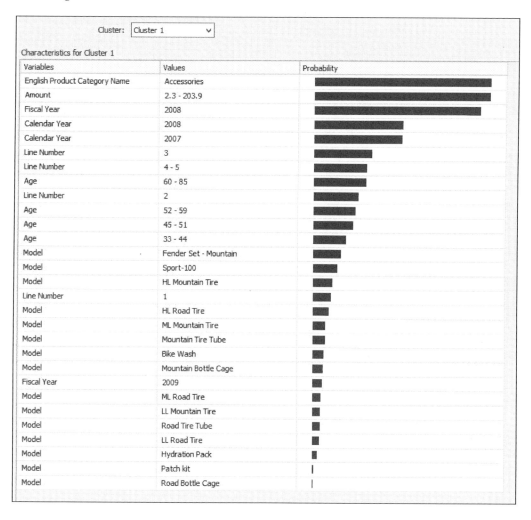

The **Probability** section shows the certainty of the variable to which a certain value will belong to this cluster. As we can see, any customer who buys some accessories will definitely belong to this group. We will now navigate to the **Cluster Discrimination** tab, as shown here:

Cluster 1:	Cluster 1	▾		Cluster 2:	Cluster 2	▾

Discrimination scores for Cluster 1 and Cluster 2

Variables	Values	Favors Cluster 1	Favors Cluster 2
Amount	27.4 - 3,578.3	▬▬▬▬▬▬▬	
Amount	2.3 - 27.4		▬▬▬▬▬▬▬▬▬
Line Number	1 - 2		▬▬▬▬
Line Number	3 - 8	▬▬▬	
Model	Water Bottle		▬
Model	Sport-100	▪	
Model	HL Mountain Tire	▪	
Model	HL Road Tire	▪	
Model	Patch kit		▪
Model	Touring Tire Tube		┃
Model	LL Road Tire		┃
Model	Fender Set - Mountain	┃	
Model	Touring Tire		┃
Model	Hydration Pack	┃	

This helps us draw a comparison between any two clusters as to which attributes and its value favors **Cluster 1** and vice versa. Let's now try to alter the data mining model by adding a few predictable attributes, as shown in the following screenshot:

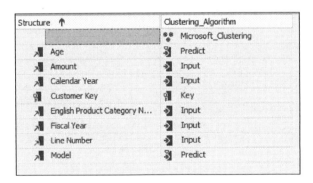

Structure ↑	Clustering_Algorithm
	Microsoft_Clustering
Age	Predict
Amount	Input
Calendar Year	Input
Customer Key	Key
English Product Category N...	Input
Fiscal Year	Input
Line Number	Input
Model	Predict

As we can see from the preceding screenshot, we have chosen **Model** as the `Predictable` attribute. We then select the value of **Model** as **Touring-2000** from the **Input Selection** tab in the **Mining Accuracy Chart** option, as shown in the following screenshot:

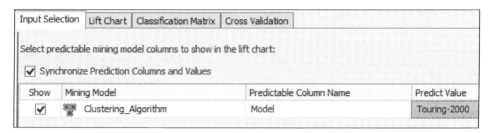

Let's look at the accuracy of the model by navigating to the **Lift Chart** tab, and referring to the lift chart in the **Mining Accuracy Chart** option:

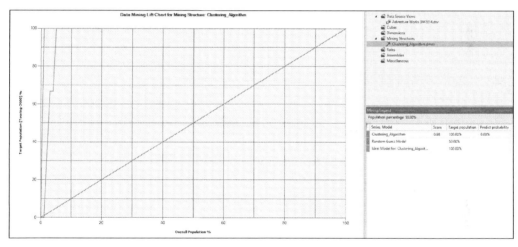

Lift chart to determine the score which in this case is 0.98

In the preceding graph, we can see that the score for the model **Touring-2000** is **0.98**. It should be noted that a lift chart in a clustering model is not really meant to determine the predictability, but to look at the accuracy of clustering, that is, the higher the score, the greater is the accuracy with which clustering happens.

For this reason, we will not look at the data mining model prediction for this model, but we'll look at the model parameters. Navigate to the following **Parameters** tab of the Microsoft Clustering algorithm, as we did for all the previous models:

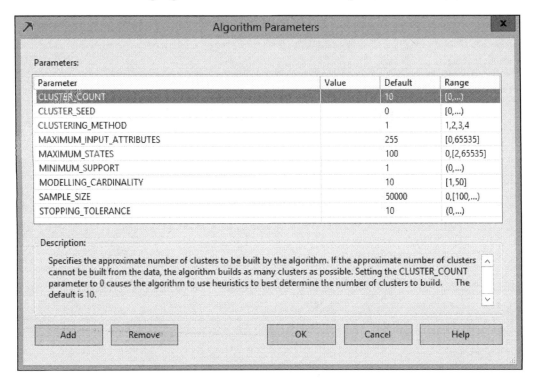

Let's discuss all the parameters in detail:

- CLUSTER_COUNT: This is the number of clusters that will be created. The default value is **10**. If we set the value to 0, the number of clusters to be created is decided based on the input data.

- CLUSTER_SEED: This is the seed number that is used to generate the clusters. The default value is **0**. Increasing the value will cause reduction in the density of clusters.

- CLUSTERING_METHOD: This is the method for the algorithm to be used. It could be **1-Scalable EM, 2-Non Scalable EM, 3-Scalable K-Means,** or **4-Non-Scalable K-Means**.

- MAXIMUM_INPUT_ATTRIBUTES: These are the number of attributes that the algorithm can hold without invoking the feature selection.

- MAXIMUM_STATES: These are the number of states for the attributes that the algorithm can support. If an attribute has more states than this, the most popular states are used.

- MINIMUM_SUPPORT: This is the number of cases required to build a cluster.

- MODELLING_CARDINALITY: This is the number of sample models constructed during the phase of creating the clusters.

- SAMPLE_SIZE: This is the case the algorithm uses for each pass of the clustering process.

- STOPPING_TOLERANCE: This is the algorithm-specific parameter and will not be used much.

More information about these parameters can be obtained from the article at `http://msdn.microsoft.com/en-IN/library/ms174879.aspx` and `http://msdn.microsoft.com/en-us/library/cc280445.aspx`.

Data Mining Extensions for the Microsoft Clustering models

Let's look at the data mining model content with the help of data mining, as shown in the following screenshot. The MSDN article at `http://msdn.microsoft.com/en-us/library/cc645761.aspx` explains each of the columns in detail. Here, the `select * from clustering_algorithm.Content;` query is executed as follows:

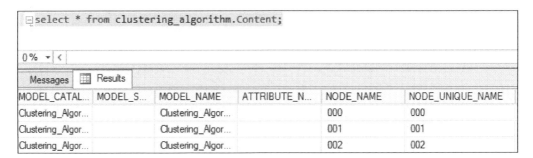

We can determine the parameters for the model by querying the DMSCHEMA_MINING_ MODELS. Add the select * from $system.DMSCHEMA_MINING_MODELS query as follows:

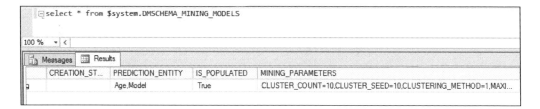

We can get the list of clusters in a data mining model using the following query:

```
SELECT NODE_NAME, NODE_CAPTION, NODE_SUPPORT, NODE_DESCRIPTION
FROM clustering_algorithm.CONTENT

WHERE NODE_TYPE = 5
```

The results of this query can be seen in the following screenshot:

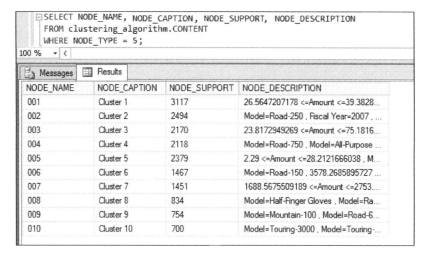

A more detailed discussion on the columns is available in the MSDN article at http://technet.microsoft.com/en-us/library/cc645761.aspx. Let's now be more specific; the following query will give us information about the nodes/clusters that have Node_support (training cases of more than 1000):

```
SELECT NODE_NAME, NODE_CAPTION, NODE_SUPPORT, NODE_DESCRIPTION
FROM clustering_algorithm.CONTENT
WHERE NODE_TYPE = 5 and Node_support>1000
```

The results of this query can be seen in the following screenshot:

We will now get more details about Cluster 2. We will look at some system-stored procedures. Although the MSDN article at `http://technet.microsoft.com/en-us/library/cc280440.aspx` does mention that we should not rely on these internal system-stored procedures, they have a backward compatibility and therefore can be used for our admin purposes. The article at `http://social.technet.microsoft.com/wiki/contents/articles/7566.a-guide-to-the-undocumented-system-stored-procedures-for-data-mining.aspx` gives a comprehensive list of the system-stored procedures for various algorithms. The following query gives us the attributes for Cluster 2 with `NodeID 002` of the model name `Clustering_Algorithm`, which has a score of greater than `0.4`:

```
CALL
System.Microsoft.AnalysisServices.System.DataMining.Clustering.Get
ClusterCharacteristics('Clustering_Algorithm', '002',0.4);
```

The other queries that will provide the same or a subset of the information are as follows:

```
CALL GetClusters('Clustering_Algorithm');
CALL System.GetClusterProfiles('Clustering_Algorithm',10,0);
```

We only show a fraction of the output window for clarity. The article at `http://msdn.microsoft.com/en-us/library/cc645772.aspx#bkmk_Nodes` gives information about `NODE_TYPE` in the `MINING_MODEL` content view.

We will now compare the two clusters with the help of a system-stored procedure. The following query gives us the discrimination between Cluster 1 and Cluster 2. For all the attributes with the probability threshold of `0.5`, we want the comparison to be rescaled (that is, normalization of values is preferred):

```
CALL
System.GetClusterDiscrimination('Clustering_Algorithm','001','002'
,0.4,true)
```

Notice the value of the score for the preceding two queries. The positive value indicates that the attribute favors Cluster1, while the negative value indicates that the attribute favors Cluster2.

Suppose we have a few values for the attributes and would like to get an idea as to the cluster in which the case would belong; the following query will help us achieve the objective:

```
SELECT Cluster(), ClusterProbability()
FROM
    [Clustering_Algorithm]
NATURAL PREDICTION JOIN
(SELECT <conditions>) AS t
```

We will elaborate the preceding query with the help of a specific example. We want to know the cluster that has a case with the value 2008 for Fiscal Year, Accessories for English Product Category Name, and 3 for amount, as shown here:

```
SELECT Cluster(), ClusterProbability()
FROM
    [Clustering_Algorithm]
NATURAL PREDICTION JOIN
(SELECT 3 as [amount],
'Accessories' as [English Product Category Name],
2008 as [Fiscal Year]) AS t
```

The result of this query can be seen in the following screenshot:

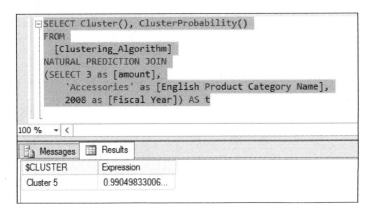

We can confirm our findings with a visual recheck of the model in SSDT, as shown in the following screenshot:

Variables	Values	Probability
English Product Category Name	Accessories	
Fiscal Year	2008	
Amount	2.3 - 203.9	
Calendar Year	2008	
Line Number	1	
Calendar Year	2007	
Line Number	2	

Here, we can see that the probability for a case to be in **Cluster 5** given the preceding set of values is quite high. Therefore, the observation is in sync with the result obtained.

The Microsoft Association algorithm

We all have been to a supermarket at some time or the other. One of the prime responsibilities of the manager of the supermarket is to sell the highest volume of products and to achieve this goal, knowledge of the purchasing patterns of the customers is required. When we know what or how our customers purchase certain products, we can suggest them products that they might be interested to buy and reorganize the store so that the items most frequently bought together are placed together. The algorithm that will help us in this endeavor is the Microsoft Association algorithm.

The input to the Microsoft Association algorithm is often in the form of a case table and a nested table. The case table consists of a unique record of each customer, while the nested table consists of multiple rows pertaining to the items purchased by the customer. The MSDN article at `http://technet.microsoft.com/en-us/library/ms175659(v=sql.110).aspx` gives a detailed explanation of nested tables.

We will now create a data mining model based on the Microsoft Association algorithm. Perform the following steps:

1. Choose any two views for our data source as **Case** and **Nested** table, as shown in the following screenshot:

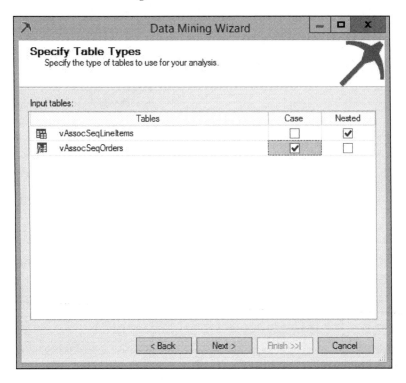

The Microsoft Association algorithm must have key columns that will identify a record uniquely. The predictable column will be in accordance with the business problem that we are trying to resolve, and the input columns will be spread across the **Case** and **Nested** tables. More details about these three requirements can be found in the **Data Required for Association Models** section of the MSDN article at `http://technet.` `microsoft.com/en-us/library/ms174916(v=sql.110).aspx`.

2. Now, select the key in the **Predictable** and **Input** columns, as shown here:

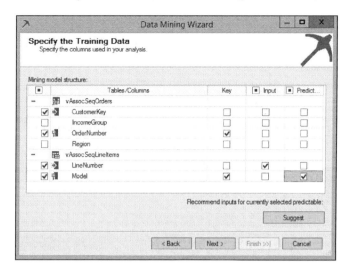

3. Click on **Next** and you will see the following screenshot, which shows the entries for the percentage of data used to check the accuracy:

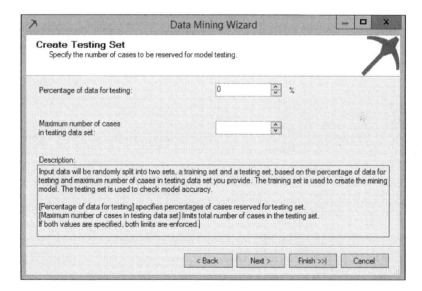

The reason why the percentage is kept as 0 is because the tools such as **Lift Chart** and the **Cross Validation Report** are not supported by the Microsoft Association algorithm. The accuracy of these algorithms can be controlled by other parameter such as MINIMUM_PROBABILITY, as explained later in this chapter.

4. Click on **Finish** and you will see the resultant data mining model, as shown here:

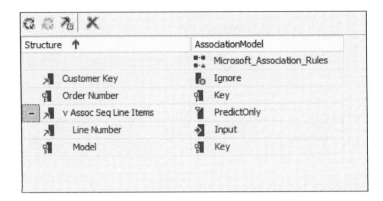

5. We then navigate to the **Rules** tab of **Mining Content Viewer**, as shown in the following screenshot:

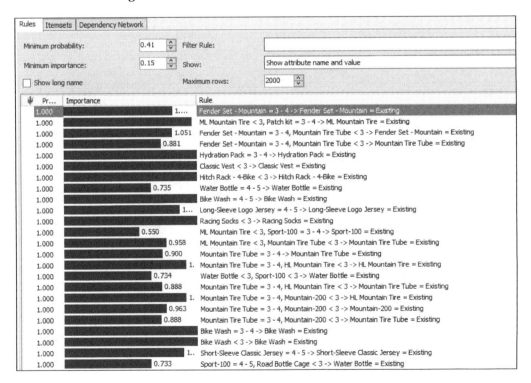

6. The association model consists of several cases and the items contained in the cases. A group of items in a case is known as an **itemset**. Click on the **ItemSets** tab of the model viewer. This gives us the view of the itemsets in the model, as shown in the following screenshot:

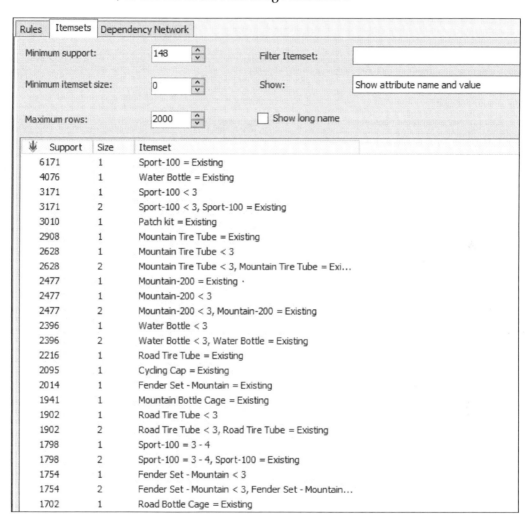

7. Navigate to the **Dependency Network** tab of the model viewer to look at the dependency network of the model. Here, we only see a part of the dependency graph, as shown in the following screenshot:

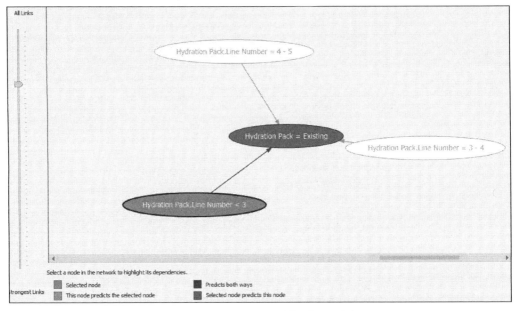

The Dependency Network for the Model

In the **Rules** tab, we will see the three columns, namely, **Probability**, **Importance**, and **Rules**. The **Probability** column shows the likelihood of the rule to occur. The **Importance** column shows the usefulness of the rule. The **Rule** column shows the occurrence of an event, for example, the sample entry `Sport-100 = 4-5, Road Bottle Cage<3->Water Bottle = Existing` has a probability of 1, which means if the value of `Sport-100` is `4-5` and there are less than 3 bottle cages, then the probability that a water bottle would also be thrown in is 1, but the usefulness of this rule is only `0.733`. This tells that there might be instances where the bottle would have been thrown in as a gift or a promotional offer.

We now turn our attention to the **Itemsets** tab, which shows the cases that support each dataset. For example, there are 6171 cases in the dataset where we have the presence of product `Sport-100`. The preceding screenshot is the one that gives us the visual information of the correlation between certain events.

We can search for any event by using the **Find Node** option, as shown in the following screenshot:

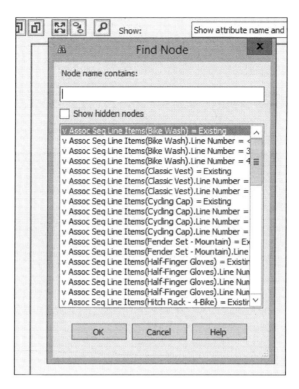

We now want to find the products that have very close associations. The answer to this lies in the **Mining Model** prediction tab, as shown in the following screenshot:

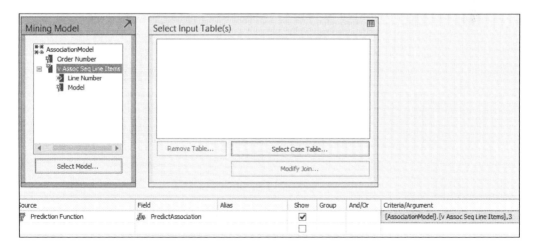

In the preceding screenshot, notice the number 3 after the comma in the **Criteria/Argument** column; this puts an upper limit on the number of products whose associations we are looking for. In this example, we want the three products that are very closely correlated with each other. The result for the preceding prediction is as follows:

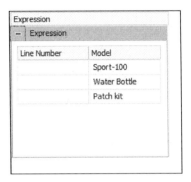

So, we can see that it does make sense for these three products to be kept in close proximity at the store, and these three products are easily accessible from the retailer website. We can extend this concept to any number of items. The following screenshot shows the prediction query for five closely associated items. Notice that we changed the value from 3 to 5.

The result is as follows:

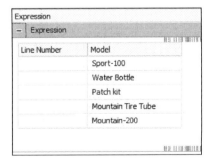

So it makes sense if we keep all the preceding items together in the retailer store.

Data Mining Extensions for the Microsoft Association models

The **Data Mining Extensions (DMX)** that will give us the result for the preceding section is as follows:

```
Select
PredictAssociation([AssociationModel].[v Assoc Seq Line Items],5)
From
[AssociationModel]
```

The DMX to get the data mining model content is as follows:

```
Select * from AssociationModel.Content;
```

The query to the information about the parameters for the data mining model is as follows:

```
select * from $system.DMSchema_mining_models;
```

The result of the preceding query is shown in the following screenshot:

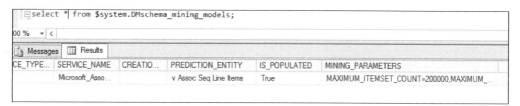

We can appropriately alter the preceding queries to get a more detailed look of the parameters or any other value. We will discuss the parameters of this model when we discuss the tuning of the algorithm in the later chapters.

The list of all the nodes together with their support (number of cases) and the probabilities can be obtained using the following query:

```
SELECT FLATTENED NODE_NAME, NODE_CAPTION,
NODE_PROBABILITY, NODE_SUPPORT,
(SELECT ATTRIBUTE_NAME FROM NODE_DISTRIBUTION) as
PurchasedProducts
FROM Associationmodel.CONTENT
WHERE NODE_TYPE = 7
```

The results of the preceding query are shown in the following screenshot:

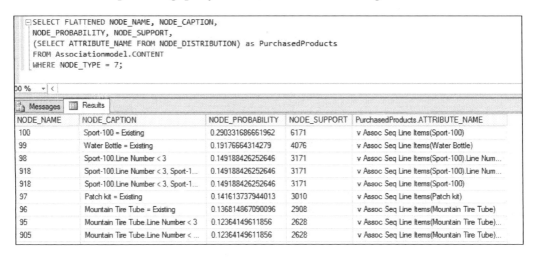

Remember when we evaluated the products that had a close association. Let's now further narrow down to the `patch kit` item and try to understand whether it has a close association with some of the products, or is it just an accessory that everybody tends to buy; we can get the answer using the following DMX:

```
SELECT TOP 100 FROM
(
SELECT FLATTENED NODE_CAPTION, NODE_SUPPORT,
(SELECT ATTRIBUTE_NAME from NODE_DISTRIBUTION
WHERE ATTRIBUTE_NAME='v Assoc Seq Line Items(patch kit)') as D
FROM Associationmodel.CONTENT
WHERE NODE_TYPE= 7
) AS Items
WHERE [D.ATTRIBUTE_NAME] <> NULL
ORDER BY NODE_SUPPORT DESC
```

The result of the preceding query is shown in the following screenshot:

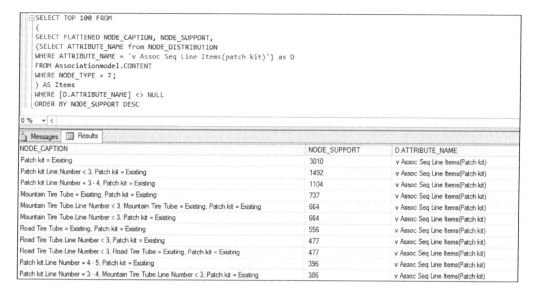

We can now clearly make out the products that have a close association with the `patch kit`. Let's now look at a very interesting observation using the prediction query designer. For now, we will frame the query for the top three. Suppose, we want to target our marketing strategy according to the customers. We want the information about the association of the products for individual customers so that we can suggest these items to them when they visit the shop. We will frame the prediction query associated products, as shown in the following screenshot:

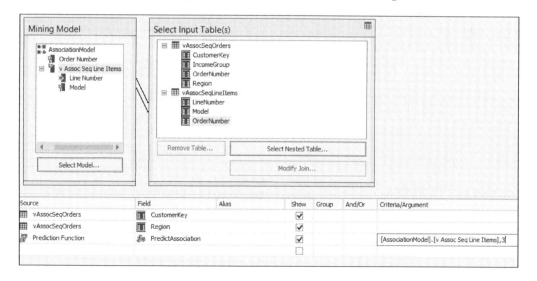

The following screenshot gives the information that we are looking for by navigating to the **Result** tab:

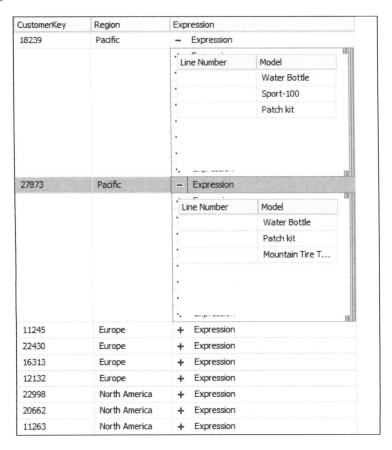

Thus, we can see that the customer with CustomerKey as 18239 will be presented with the various models, namely, **Water Bottle**, **Sport-100**, and **Patch kit**.

The query for the preceding prediction can be obtained from the **Query** tab, which is as follows:

```
{ ('SELECT
[CustomerKey],
[Region],
[OrderNumber]
From
[dbo].[vAssocSeqOrders]
```

```
ORDER BY
[OrderNumber]')}
APPEND
({OPENQUERY([AssociationDataSource].
'SELECT
[LineNumber],
[Model],
[OrderNumber]
FROM
[dbo].[vAssocSeqLineItems]
ORDER BY
[OrderNumber]'})
RELATE
[OrderNumber] TO [OrderNumber])
AS
[vAssocSeqLineItems] AS t
ON
[AssociationModel].[v Assoc Seq Line Items].[Line
Number]=t.[vAssocSeqLineItems].[LineNumber]
AND
[AssociationModel].[v Assoc Seq Line
Items].[Model]=t.[vAssocSeqLineItems].[Model]
```

The article at `http://msdn.microsoft.com/en-us/library/ms131996.aspx` explains all the prediction functions that are available in SQL Server Data Mining. The articles at `http://msdn.microsoft.com/en-us/library/ms174916.aspx` and `http://msdn.microsoft.com/en-us/library/cc280428.aspx` provide additional technical details about the Microsoft Association algorithm.

Summary

In this chapter, we looked at the details of the two data mining algorithms, namely, the Microsoft Clustering algorithm and the Microsoft Association algorithm. We discussed their properties, their parameters, and the effect of their change on the algorithm behavior. In the next chapter, we will discuss the remaining two categories of algorithms, namely, the Sequence and the Regression Models.

7
Sequence and Regression Models

In the previous chapter, we looked at the clustering and the association rules algorithms, which basically gave us an idea of how to identify associated groups in our dataset. Let's now consider a problem of a marketing manager of a popular online retailer site. Here, there are various categories of products sold, including books, magazines, electronics, cookware, office products, and so on. Every day, thousands of web customers come to the site, navigating to different domains of the portal of the retail shop. In a physical shop, these departments and products that attract most customers and the customer interactions on various products are easily identifiable. In a virtual store, the manager cannot see the customers. However, it is important to learn more about his customers to provide them with better services. It is important to determine how the customers are using the site and the list of products for which they have shown interest. There is also a need to know the natural groups among these customers based on their navigation patterns; for example, one group of customers shop for all sorts of products on the website, whereas some visit only certain categories of books and magazines.

This information not only gives the manager a clear picture of his customers' behaviors in the virtual shop, but also allows him/her to provide personalized shopping guidance to every customer based on the customer's profile. The Microsoft Sequence Clustering algorithm can be used to analyze navigation sequences and organize sequences in natural groups based on their similarities. The manager also needs to understand the sales trend of certain products so that adequate quantities of the product can be stored. The Microsoft Linear Regression algorithm will help predict the sales of the products based on the previous sales data.

In this chapter, we will cover the following topics:

- The Microsoft Sequence Clustering algorithm and the associated data mining Extensions
- The Microsoft Time Series algorithm

The Microsoft Sequence Clustering algorithm

Now that we now have a proper understanding of the situation wherein we will use the Microsoft Sequence Clustering algorithm, we will continue using the same business problem for the AdventureWorks site.

We will use the same case and nested tables for our data mining model that we used in the previous chapters, namely, **vAssocSeqLineItems** and **vAssocSeqOrders**, as shown in the following screenshot:

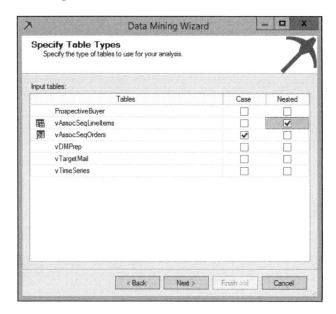

Select the key column that will uniquely identify the records in the **Case** table and will help identify the related records in the **Nested** table. A sequence column will identify the events that occur in a sequence. The nonsequence columns contain more information about the sequence such as the web page name, URLs visited, and so on. The predictable column is selected based on the sequence we are interested in.

As we are interested in the sequence of models, we choose **Model** as the **Predictable** column, as shown in the following screenshot:

After passing through all the stages of the data mining model creation as done in the previous chapters, the model is created as shown here:

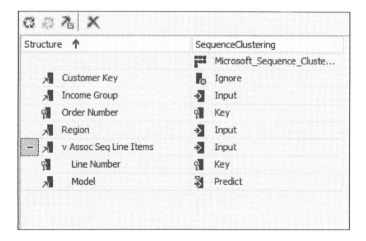

The view of the sequence cluster from the **Cluster Profiles** tab is shown in the following screenshot. Notice an additional row with **Variables** tagged as **Model.samples**.

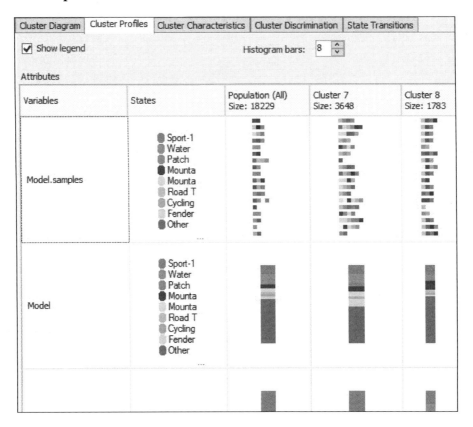

The row labeled **Model.samples** shows the most commonly occurring sequences in a cluster. The row labeled **Model** shows the probability of the model occurring in the clusters. We can see from the preceding histogram that **Sport-1** exists as the first element of every sequence; hence, it has the most probability of being chosen by the customer.

The cluster diagram is similar to the clustering model in the sense that it shows the cluster of data that has close resemblance to one another. As we can see in the following screenshot, **Shading Variable** is chosen to be **Model** and **State** as **Bike Wash**. The color of a cluster is the indication of the probability of customers in that cluster to buy bike wash.

Thus, we can see that the customers classified in **Cluster 15** have the maximum probability of buying a bike wash.

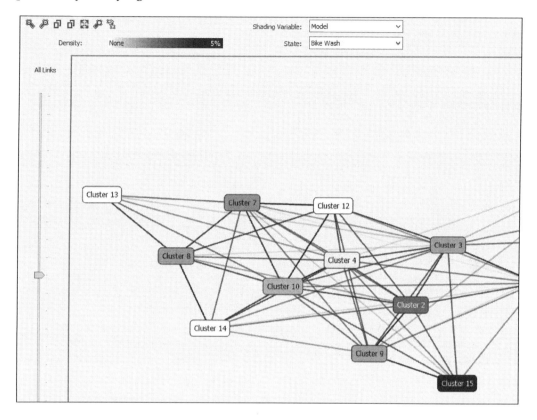

The following **Cluster Characteristics** tab helps us understand the values of different variables in **Cluster 1**:

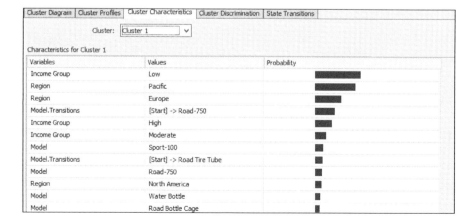

The cluster discrimination is no different from other models so we will move on to the **State Transitions** tab, as shown in the following screenshot:

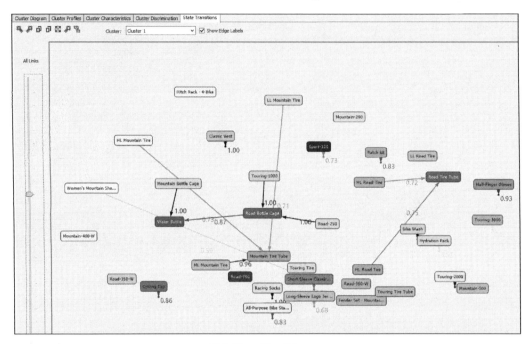

State Transition Diagram

The Microsoft Sequence Clustering algorithm uses Markov models to identify the sequences and determine the probability of sequences. A Markov model stores the transitions between different states. The Microsoft Sequence Clustering algorithm uses n-order Markov chains. The number of orders in a Markov chain determines the number of states used to determine the probability of the current state. In a first order Markov model, the probability of the current state depends only on the previous state, whereas in a second order Markov chain, the probability of a state depends on the previous two states, and so on. Every Markov chain has a transition matrix that stores the transitions for each combination of states. The size of the matrix increases exponentially with the increase in the states in the Markov chain. The Microsoft Sequence Clustering algorithm performs cluster decomposition to separate clusters based on sequences and other attributes because the number of clusters created are more than that of other clustering algorithms, and it might become really difficult to interpret the final results with such a large number of clusters. The article at `http://msdn.microsoft.com/en-us/library/cc645866.aspx` provides more information on the implementation of the Microsoft Sequence Clustering model.

In the preceding screenshot, we can see that if a customer buys **Road-250**, there is every possibility of him buying a road bottle cage. Also, there is an 87 percent probability that he will buy a water bottle too. We see that **Cycling Cap** starts with a period indicating the beginning of the sequence, whereas **Mountain-500** ends with a period indicating it to be at the end of the sequence.

As we are only looking for patterns here, the mining accuracy chart will really not provide us with any useful information. So we move on to the **Mining Model** prediction tab and try to get some insight in terms of the items that have the probability of being brought together in a sequence.

The following screenshot shows the **Mining Model** prediction tab for the Microsoft Sequence Clustering model:

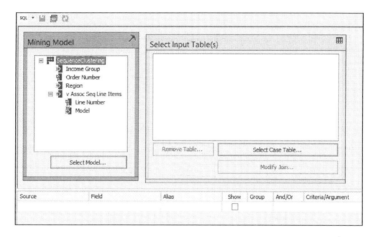

We then drag the **vAssocSeqOrders (dbo)** view to the **Input Table** section by selecting the **Select Case** table, as shown in the following screenshot:

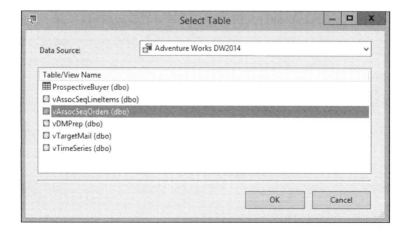

We then select **vAssocSeqLineItems,** as shown here:

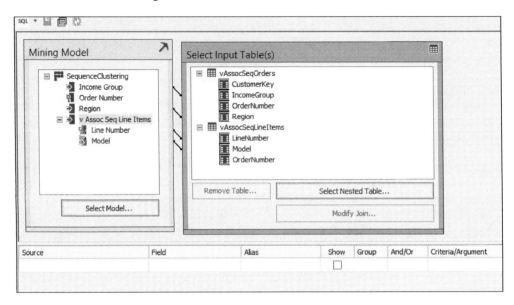

We then drag the **vAssocSeqLineItems** from the **Mining Model** dialog box and **Region** from the **Select Input Table(s)** section and drop them in the query designer section, as shown in the following screenshot:

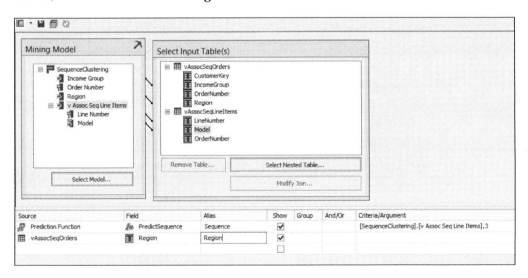

The [SequenceClustering].[v Assoc Seq Line Items],3 criteria will give us the output as the prediction of the number of items has three sequences. The result of this query is as follows:

Expand any one sequence and you will see the following result:

Sequence			Region
− Sequence			Pacific
$SEQUENCE	Line Number	Model	
1		Water Bottle	
2		Sport-100	
3		Half-Finger Glo…	

We might also want to see the sequence for a particular region or for a particular product. As we want to predict a sequence for a single case and want to supply the values for a region directly in the query, we can use the singleton query here. The article at `http://msdn.microsoft.com/en-us/library/hh213169.aspx` provides more information about the type of prediction queries. So, let's switch over to the **Singleton query** editor, as shown in the following screenshot:

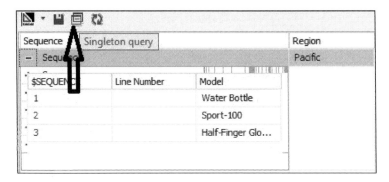

A dialog box will warn us that we would lose our query if we switch windows; we can safely click on **OK**. We again drag the **vAssocSeqLineItems** on to the grid, and then select **Region** as **North America**, as shown in the following screenshot:

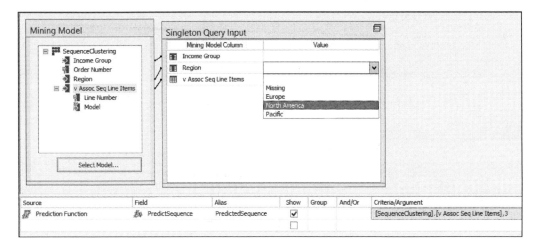

We will then switch to the **Results** pane in order to see the result, as shown here:

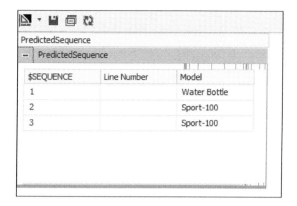

Now, let's get the sequence of products following the purchase of a few products. For this, we will have to return to the **Singleton Query Input** dialog box and click on ellipses next to the **vAssocSeqLineItems**. This will bring up the **Nested Table Input** window, as shown in the following screenshot:

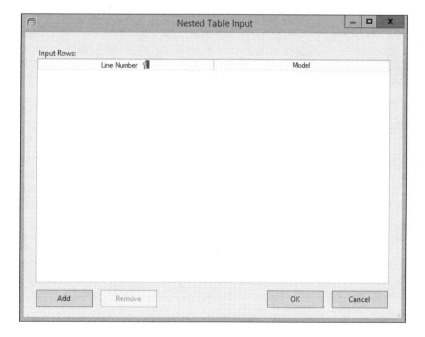

We will now add some value to the model by clicking on the **Add** button and selecting any value of the model from the drop-down menu, as shown here:

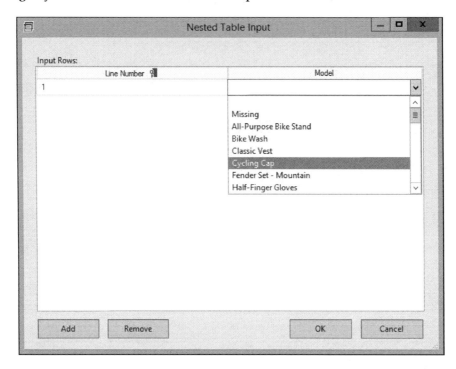

Select **Touring Tire Tube** from the drop-down menu, click on **OK**, and then click on **Results**. We will see the following result:

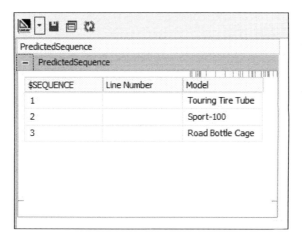

We can now see how the Microsoft Sequence Clustering algorithm helps us predict the sequence of events in any organization. All we need to do is collate the data from various events and segregate it into the case table and nested table, as is the case with **vAssocSeqOrders** and **vAssocSeqLineItems**.

Let's discuss some important parameters for the Microsoft Sequence Clustering algorithm. We already discussed how to get to the algorithm parameter screen for the other models. So, we will only discuss the parameters here:

- CLUSTER_COUNT: This parameter specifies the approximate number of clusters that will be built by the algorithm. The default is 10, but we can alter the number of clusters that will be created. We already saw the number of clusters created for the model under consideration.

- MINIMUM_SUPPORT: This parameter specifies the number of cases that are required to form a cluster.

- MAXIMUM_SEQUENCE_STATES: This parameter specifies the number of states that a sequence can have.

- MAXIMUM_STATES: This parameter specifies the number of states for nonsequential attributes. We can see both sequential and nonsequential attributes in the **State Transitions** tab.

The article at http://msdn.microsoft.com/en-us/library/cc645866.aspx provides us with more information about these parameters.

Data Mining Extensions for the Microsoft Sequence Clustering models

Let's now look at the **Data Mining Extensions (DMX)** for the Microsoft Sequence Clustering algorithm. Use the following code to query the model content view in the data mining model:

```
Select * from sequenceclustering.content;
```

We will now query the parameters for the models using the following code:

```
Select MINING_PARAMETERS from $system.DMSCHEMA_MINING_MODELS;
```

The following query will help us see the sequence at the model level:

```
SELECT FLATTENED NODE_UNIQUE_NAME,
(SELECT ATTRIBUTE_VALUE AS [Product 1],
[Support] AS [Sequence Support],
```

```
[Probability] AS [Sequence Probability]
FROM NODE_DISTRIBUTION) AS t
FROM [SequenceClustering].CONTENT
Where NODE_TYPE = 13
AND [PARENT_UNIQUE_NAME] = 0;
```

The Node_type = 13 node is the top node of the Markov model and PARENT_UNIQUE_NAME = 0 is used to list the direct descendent node of the top node of the model. The article at http://technet.microsoft.com/en-us/library/cc645772.aspx gives more detailed information about NODE_TYPES and the different columns of the view. The results of the preceding query are as follows:

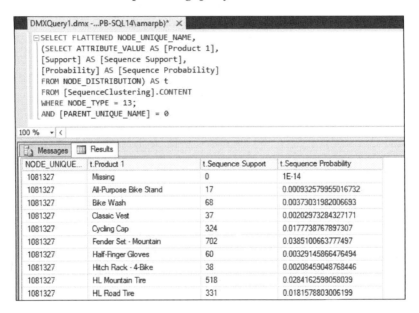

The attribute values are stored in alphabetical order; therefore, we can identify the sequence of a product easily with the preceding query. So **Touring Tire** is actually **Sequence Number 32** in the preceding screenshot. Let's try to find out the sequence after **Touring Tire**.

We will begin by getting **NODE_UNIQUE_NAME** using the following query:

```
SELECT NODE_UNIQUE_NAME
FROM [SequenceClustering].CONTENT
WHERE NODE_DESCRIPTION = 'Transition row for sequence state 32'
AND [PARENT_UNIQUE_NAME] = '1081327';
```

The result of this query is seen in the following screenshot:

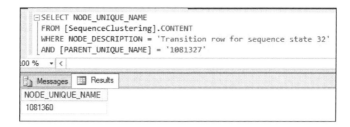

We can then use `NODE_UNIQUE_NAME` to get the sequence, as follows:

```
SELECT FLATTENED
(SELECT ATTRIBUTE_VALUE AS [Product 2],
[Support] AS [P2 Support],
[Probability] AS [P2 Probability],
FROM NODE_DISTRIBUTION) AS t
FROM [SequenceClustering].CONTENT
Where NODE_UNIQUE_NAME = '1081360';
```

The results of the preceding query are seen in the following screenshot:

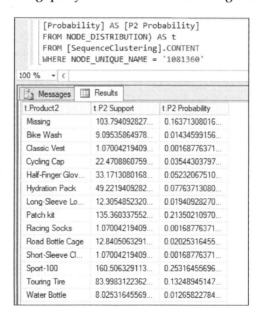

To make predictions, we can always get the initial query from the query designer and then make appropriate modifications to the query conditions. This is applicable to any data mining model. The article at `http://msdn.microsoft.com/en-us/library/cc645869.aspx` details the DMX for sequence clustering models.

The Microsoft Time Series algorithm

The Microsoft Time Series algorithm provides the capabilities to predict the value of continuous variables, such as sales for the next year or subsequent years. The algorithm has both short-term and long-term prediction capabilities. The short-term value prediction capability, which involves predicting the immediate next value, is provided by the **Autoregressive Tree Model for Time Series Analysis (ARTXP)**, and the long-term prediction capability is provided by the **Autoregressive Integrated Moving Average Algorithm (ARIMA)**. The Microsoft Time Series algorithm also has the capability to provide the prediction for one product given the behavior of the other product whose trend is related to the first product. This prediction is popularly known as cross prediction. The article at `http://msdn.microsoft.com/en-us/library/bb677216.aspx` provides more details pertaining to the implementation of the algorithm.

The following screenshot of the data mining model is constructed in the Microsoft Time Series Data Mining model and uses the **vTimeSeries** view, which is a part of the AdventureWorksDW2014 database as the dataset:

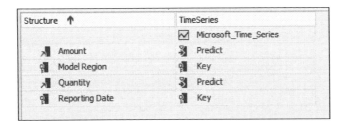

The data mining model viewer for this model is shown in the following screenshot:

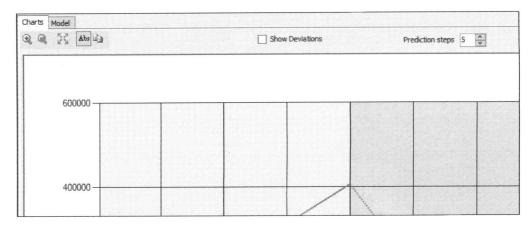

In the preceding screenshot, we can see the two tabs, namely, the **Charts** and **Model** tabs. The **Charts** tab gives us the value of the predictable column over a time frame. The *y* axis gives the value of the attribute, while the *x* axis gives the value of the time frame. The following screenshot shows the chart for the predicted value of certain products:

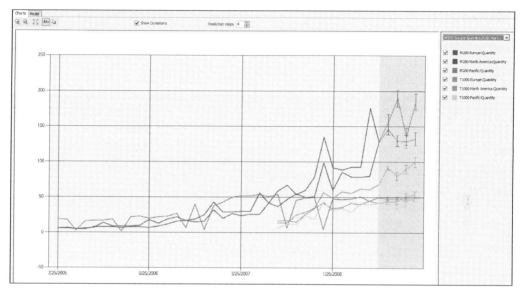

Sample Prediction chart showing the predicted value of certain products

We can add or subtract the products by checking or unchecking the values from the drop-down menu on the right-hand side of the graph. As we can see in the preceding screenshot, we have selected **Show Deviations** and the **Prediction steps** option is set to **4**. The **Show Deviations** option enables bars to be displayed on the screen that will tell us how accurate the prediction for a product is. The prediction steps will show us the prediction for the upcoming *n* number of time frames, *n* being the prediction steps. We will now look at the **Model** tab where the forecasting model can be viewed in the form of a tree. The tree can have a single branch or multiple branches depending on the complexity of the time series. The little diamonds represent continuous numbers. The bar represents the range of the attributes. The diamond is centered on the mean for the node, and the width of the diamond represents the variance of the attribute at that node. The article at `http://msdn.microsoft.com/en-us/library/ms166988.aspx` provides more details about the **Model** and the **Chart** tabs.

Here, we choose the value of **Tree** as **M200 North America: Amount, Background** as **All Cases**, and **Default Expansion** as **All Levels**:

Decision Tree for the model

There are 12 distinct values in the table and we are looking for the two predictions, namely, **Amount** and **Quantity**, so we can have *12*2 = 24* trees, as shown in the following drop-down menu of **Tree**:

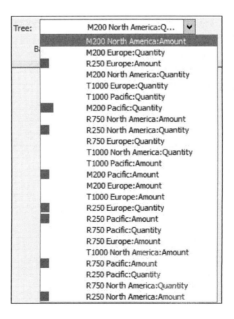

Let's select the first value **M200 Europe: Quantity**; we can see that there is only one histogram shown without any splits. The reason being that the trend found in the model is consistent and we can use this model for our predictions. If, however, there is a split, this signifies a greater amount of complexity in the time series, so the tree is split into multiple branches each with a separate time segment. The following screenshot shows a single tree:

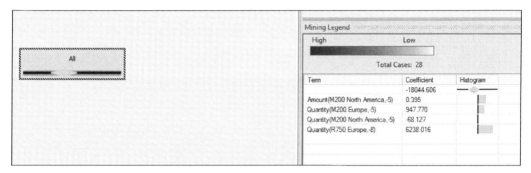

The single tree

The split tree can be seen in the following screenshot:

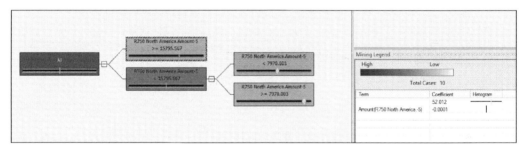

The split tree for the model

Let's predict certain values with the help of this model. We will move on to the **Mining Model** prediction tab and then put the values in the grid, as shown in the following screenshot:

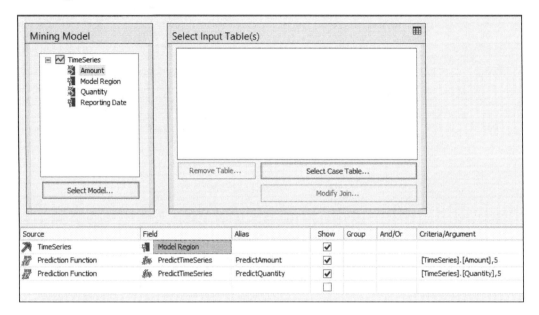

Move on to the **Query** screen and enter the following query:

```
SELECT
[TimeSeries].[Model Region],
(PredictTimeSeries([TimeSeries].[Amount],5)) As [PredictAmount],
(PredictTimeSeries([TimeSeries].[Quantity],5)) As
[PredictQuantity]
From
[TimeSeries]
```

The results of this query are shown in the following screenshot:

Model Region	PredictAmount		PredictQuantity	
M200 Europe	− PredictAmount		− PredictQuantity	
	$TIME	**Amount**	**$TIME**	**Quantity**
	7/25/2008 12:...	311847.04453...	7/25/2008 12:...	146
	8/25/2008 12:...	307939.92044...	8/25/2008 12:...	130
	9/25/2008 12:...	320901.83620...	9/25/2008 12:...	129
	10/25/2008 12...	324481.16740...	10/25/2008 12...	133
	11/25/2008 12...	301242.03639...	11/25/2008 12...	142
M200 North America	− PredictAmount		− PredictQuantity	
	$TIME	**Amount**	**$TIME**	**Quantity**
	7/25/2008 12:...	363125.21882...	7/25/2008 12:...	156
	8/25/2008 12:...	440970.54424...	8/25/2008 12:...	190
	9/25/2008 12:...	316220.11209...	9/25/2008 12:...	136
	10/25/2008 12...	424586.03979...	10/25/2008 12...	185
	11/25/2008 12...	486661.20002...	11/25/2008 12...	209
M200 Pacific	+ PredictAmount		+ PredictQuantity	
R250 Europe	+ PredictAmount		+ PredictQuantity	
R250 North America	+ PredictAmount		+ PredictQuantity	
R250 Pacific	+ PredictAmount		+ PredictQuantity	
R750 Europe	+ PredictAmount		+ PredictQuantity	
R750 North America	+ PredictAmount		+ PredictQuantity	
R750 Pacific	+ PredictAmount		+ PredictQuantity	
T1000 Europe	+ PredictAmount		+ PredictQuantity	
T1000 North America	+ PredictAmount		+ PredictQuantity	
T1000 Pacific	+ PredictAmount		+ PredictQuantity	

Although we succeeded in predicting the values for the upcoming year with the existing data, more data is continuously added and we might need to look at the change in predictions because of the addition of new data.

We can create a table with random sales data using the following set of scripts:

- The following query will create a table of the structure similar to the `vTimeSeries` view:

```
select * into SalesDataUpdated from vTimeSeries where 1 > 2
```

- This following query will create a stored procedure to enter data into the `SalesDataUpdated` table:

```
create procedure insertintoSales @startyear int,@endyear
int
as
declare @productName table
(    productkey int,
      productName nvarchar(56)
)
insert into @productName
select 0,'Mountain-100'
UNION ALL select 1,'Road-150'
UNION ALL select 2,'Road-650'
UNION ALL  select 3,'Touring-1000'
declare @regiontable table
(    regionkey int,
        region nvarchar(56)
)
insert into @regiontable
select 0,'Europe'
UNION ALL  select 1,'North America'
UNION ALL  select 2,'Pacific'
declare @date char(8);
declare @product int=0;
declare @region int=0;
declare @month int=1;
declare @monthmod nvarchar(2);
declare @random int;
declare @lower int=1;
declare @upper int =100;
declare @productvar nvarchar(56);
declare @regionvar nvarchar(56);
declare @yearvar int=@startyear;
```

```
while @yearvar<@endyear begin
set @product=0;
while @product<4 begin
    set @region=0;
while @region<3 begin
    set @month=1;
while @month<13 begin
    select @productvar=productName from @productName where
productkey=@product;
    select @regionvar=region from @regiontable where
regionkey=@region;
set @monthmod=concat(replicate('0', 2 - len(@month)),cast
(@month as varchar));
    set @date =concat(@yearvar,@monthmod,'25');
    select @random=ROUND(((@upper-@lower-
      1)*rand()+@lower),0);
    insert into [dbo].[SalesDataUpdated]
    SELECT
CASE @productvar WHEN 'Mountain-100' THEN 'M200' WHEN
'Road-150' THEN 'R250' WHEN 'Road-650' THEN 'R750' WHEN
'Touring-1000' THEN 'T1000' END + ' ' + @regionvar AS
ModelRegion,
    CONVERT(Integer, @yearvar) * 100 + CONVERT(Integer,
@month) AS TimeIndex,@random as
Quantity,abs(cast(CAST(NEWID() AS VARBINARY(4))as
int)/100.0) as Amount,@yearvar as CalendarYear,
@month as Month,convert(datetime,@date) as ReportingDate;
    set @month = @month+1;
    end
    set @region = @region+1;
    end
    set @product = @product+1;
end
    set @yearvar = @yearvar+1;
end
go
```

- We can execute the stored procedure from the year 2005 to 2008 as follows:

```
exec insertintoSales 2005, 2008
```

We now have the updated data (though hypothetical) in the **SalesDataUpdated** table. Let's use this data to get the updated prediction. Select the case table, as shown in the following screenshot:

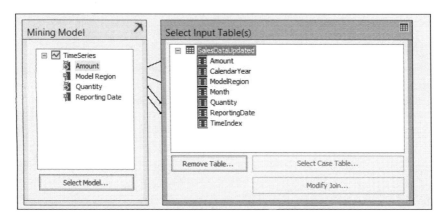

Let's check the mapping of the case table and the model by clicking on any of the connecting lines between **Mining Model** and **Select Input Table(s)**, as shown in the preceding screenshot. Clicking on the **Modify Mapping** option will open a separate dialog box, as shown here:

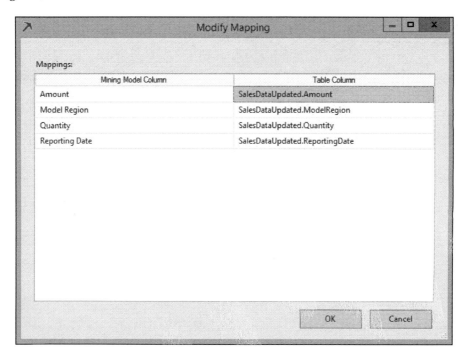

We now add the EXTEND_MODEL_CASES clause to the query in order to add new data to the original data set, as shown in the following screenshot. The article at http://msdn.microsoft.com/en-us/library/ms132167.aspx provides details about the other clauses that can be added.

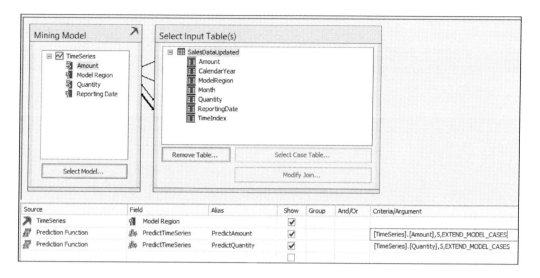

We can see that the results are still the same. For this, we need to specify the time slice after the original data, stating that we will need the results. For example, if we need the results from October to December, we will change the query, as shown in the following screenshot:

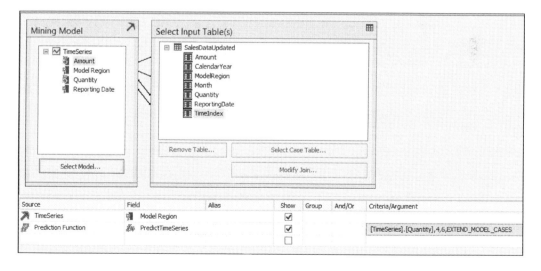

The result of this query can be seen in the following screenshot:

Model Region	Expression	
M200 Europe	– Expression	

$TIME	Quantity
10/25/2008 12...	9
11/25/2008 12...	73
12/25/2008 12...	57

Model Region		Expression
M200 North Am...	+	Expression
M200 Pacific	+	Expression
R250 Europe	+	Expression
R250 North Am...	+	Expression
R250 Pacific	+	Expression
R750 Europe	+	Expression
R750 North Am...	+	Expression
R750 Pacific	+	Expression
T1000 Europe	+	Expression
T1000 North A...	+	Expression
T1000 Pacific	+	Expression

Let's look at another aspect of the prediction model: the cross prediction. We saw in the original model that the sales of **M200 in Europe** are skyrocketing, while that of **T1000** are not that great, which is illustrated in the following screenshot:

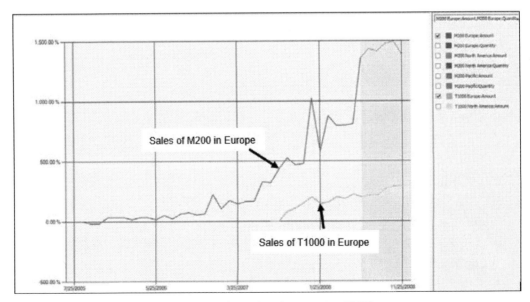

Comparison of the sales of M200 versus T1000

Let's now look at the data that we have in the **TimeSeries** view for **M200** and **T1000** using the following query:

```
SELECT
[ModelRegion]
,[Timeindex]
,[Quantity]
,[Amount]
,[CalendarYear]
,[Month]
,[ReportingDate]
FROM [AdventureWorksDW2014].[dbo].[vTimeSeries] where
[ModelRegion] in ('M200 Europe' , 'T1000 Europe') order by
[CalendarYear],Month
```

The results of this query are shown in the following screenshot:

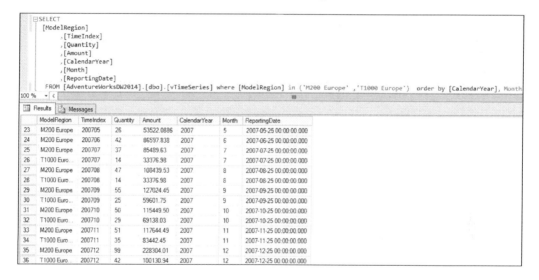

Now, we can see that we don't have the same range of data for both of these products, so the trends might not give the actual comparison. A solution to this anomaly is to create a generalized model that will contain the values for amount and quantity in totality and then apply this generalized model to predict the value for the individual product.

The easiest way we can create the generalized model is by using the **TimeSeries** view and summing `Quantity` and `Amount` over the entire European region using the following script:

```
select ReportingDate,
SUM([Quantity]) as SumQty, AVG([Quantity]) AS AvgQty,
SUM([Amount]) AS SumAmt, AVG([Amount]) AS AvgAmt,
'All Regions and Models' AS [Region] into MainTotal
FROM dbo.vTimeSeries
GROUP BY ReportingDate;
```

The following query will help us see the data in the `MainTotal` table:

```
Select * from MainTotal;
```

The results of this query are shown in the following screenshot:

	ReportingDate	SumQty	AvgQty	SumAmt	AvgAmt	Region
1	2007-12-25 00:00:00.000	605	50	1147780.95	95648.4125	All Regions and Models
2	2006-10-25 00:00:00.000	208	23	394381.0458	43820.1162	All Regions and Models
3	2007-02-25 00:00:00.000	244	27	461078.0856	51230.8984	All Regions and Models
4	2006-07-25 00:00:00.000	236	26	483357.7175	53706.413	All Regions and Models
5	2005-09-25 00:00:00.000	146	16	473943.0312	52660.3368	All Regions and Models
6	2006-11-25 00:00:00.000	172	19	314085.9012	34898.4334	All Regions and Models
7	2005-12-25 00:00:00.000	235	26	755527.8914	83947.5434	All Regions and Models
8	2007-06-25 00:00:00.000	281	31	514781.7281	57197.9697	All Regions and Models
9	2008-05-25 00:00:00.000	653	54	1239580.35	103298.3625	All Regions and Models
10	2007-01-25 00:00:00.000	219	24	413854.2343	45983.8038	All Regions and Models
11	2005-08-25 00:00:00.000	156	17	506191.6912	56243.5212	All Regions and Models
12	2007-05-25 00:00:00.000	282	31	509749.377	56638.8196	All Regions and Models
13	2006-03-25 00:00:00.000	199	22	644135.2022	71570.578	All Regions and Models
14	2007-08-25 00:00:00.000	306	25	572438.98	47703.2483	All Regions and Models
15	2006-04-25 00:00:00.000	207	23	663692.2868	73743.5874	All Regions and Models
16	2007-09-25 00:00:00.000	364	30	695827.00	57985.5833	All Regions and Models
17	2005-11-25 00:00:00.000	169	18	543993.4058	60443.7117	All Regions and Models

We also create another table that will contain the value for **T1000 Europe** by using the following script:

```
SELECT ReportingDate,ModelRegion,Quantity,Amount into t1000europe
FROM dbo.vTimeSeries
WHERE (ModelRegion = N'T1000 Europe')
```

Let's now create a new mining model with this table and name it
`AggregatesTimeSeries`. The structure of this model is shown in the
following screenshot:

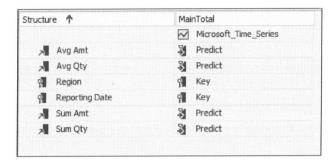

Let's navigate to the **Mining Model Column** tab and manage the mappings,
as shown here:

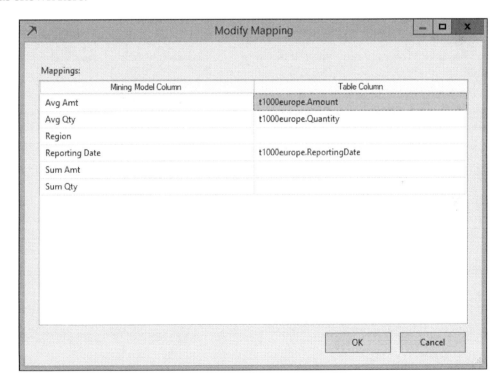

Now, let's get the prediction query in place, as shown in the following screenshot. The article at `http://msdn.microsoft.com/en-us/library/cc879284.aspx` gives information about the `REPLACE_MODEL_CASES` that we have used.

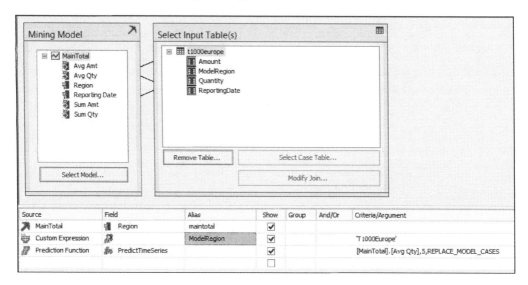

The results are shown in the following screenshot:

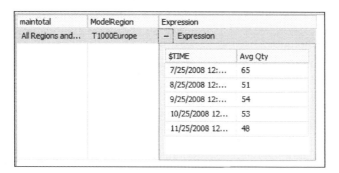

As these values are over and above the originally predicted values, we can plot these values alongside the original values. However, see that we not only preserve the original trend, but also make it better.

Summary

In this chapter, we discussed the Microsoft Sequence Clustering algorithm, which helped us determine the items that are most probable to be bought together and in a particular sequence. We were not only able to predict the items that will be bought, but also got an idea of how to modify the page wise navigation of the website so that it provides a better user experience. The Microsoft Time Series algorithm helped us predict certain values of the sales of certain commodities for a future date and time with the data of the previous sales. In the next chapter, we will look at the data mining capabilities provided to us by Excel and HDInsight. We will also explore its functionalities and perform a simple data mining activity using the Excel data mining add-in and Mahout in HDInsight.

8

Data Mining Using Excel and Big Data

In the previous chapters, we used various data mining algorithms to find the data that we were looking for. With Microsoft Excel becoming more and more powerful in terms of performing data analysis and having connectivity capabilities to many data sources, an addition of the data mining capabilities is only a logical enhancement to its capabilities.

The state of data today is aptly described by volume, variety, and velocity. Volume describes the quantity of data generated, variety describes the type of data that is generated from different sources, and velocity is the rate at which the data gets generated. The most common examples are social media platforms such as Facebook, Twitter, and so on, where we have posts and tweets from millions of people on a daily basis. These comprise of photos, audio files, video files, texts, and so on. These posts and tweets take some several terabytes of space in the data centers of Facebook and Twitter. Traditional **relational database management system (RDBMS)** systems are pushed to their limits in such a scenario. Hence, there's a need to develop a system that can handle the data in such versatile date in huge quantities. Thus, NoSQL and Big Data were born, and Mahout is one of the open source projects that provide the data mining capabilities to the Big Data platform. Machine Learning is another solution that uses the power of Big Data in the backend while providing the ability to learn from previous analytical observations, continuously improving its efficiency and effectiveness. We will now cover Machine Learning just to get the users started with Microsoft Azure Machine Learning.

In this chapter, we will cover the following topics:

- Data mining using Microsoft Excel
- Data mining using Big Data

Data mining using Microsoft Excel

The data mining plugin for Microsoft Excel provides us with the ability to build a data mining model and handle a wide range of data from various data sources. The following are a few features provided by this add-in:

- Analyze how values in a data column are influenced by values in all the other columns

- Detect groups of rows with similar characteristics

- Automatically populate a column with values based on a few examples you provide

- Perform forecasting on a time series

- Find rows that are unlike most other rows (interesting or anomalous)

- Perform a scenario (goal-seeking or what-if) analysis

- Create a powerful (yet easy-to-use) prediction calculator

- Perform shopping basket analysis and identify cross-sales opportunities

The article at `http://msdn.microsoft.com/en-in/library/dn282385.aspx` provides more details about the data mining add-in for Excel. The link to download the data mining plugin for Excel 2007 is `http://www.microsoft.com/en-us/download/details.aspx?id=7294` and for Excel 2010 is `http://www.microsoft.com/en-us/download/details.aspx?id=29061`.

Let's install the data mining plugin for Excel 2013 from the link at `http://www.microsoft.com/en-us/download/details.aspx?id=35578`, which will provide both the x86 and x64 versions of the add-in. Install the plugin that matches the version of Microsoft Office installed on your computer. If you have 64-bit Microsoft Office, then install the x64 plugin of the data mining plugin. However, if you have a 32-bit version of Microsoft Office, then install the x86 plugin. The advantage of using the x64 plugin is that it allows you to work with larger datasets. We will install the x64 plugin for our example. We will need an instance of SQL Server Analysis Services installed and running in our network (or on our machine). Analysis Services is included in the Microsoft SQL Server installation media, so you will probably need to ask your database administrator to point you to an Analysis Services installation. If Analysis Services is not available, you can download a free evaluation copy of Microsoft SQL Server from `http://www.microsoft.com/en-us/evalcenter/evaluate-sql-server-2014`.

Once successfully installed, we should be able to see the **DATA MINING** option available in the menu bar, as shown in the following screenshot:

The article at `http://www.bettersolutions.com/excel/ECC108/YB610620882.htm` provides information about the various tabs that we see in the preceding screenshot. When working with data mining, we will only work in the **Data Mining** tab. We will now create a data mining model using the Decision Tree algorithm.

Perform the following steps:

1. Make a connection using the **Connection** option, as shown with a circle in the following screenshot:

Default connection initialized to localhost

2. Click on the connection icon, and then click on **New** to create a new connection. The details that we fed to get the example going are shown in the following screenshot:

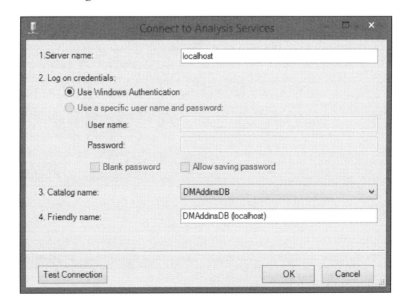

3. Enter `localhost` in the **Server name** field as the Analysis Services Server is on the same machine. Enter the details here and click on **OK**.

4. We will now create a sample model on the **SQL Server Analysis Services (SSAS)** server by clicking on the **Advanced** tab, which provides us with the two options, namely, **Create Mining Structure** and **Add Model to Structure**; click on **Create Mining Structure**. This brings up the mining wizard, as shown in the following screenshot; we then click on **Next**:

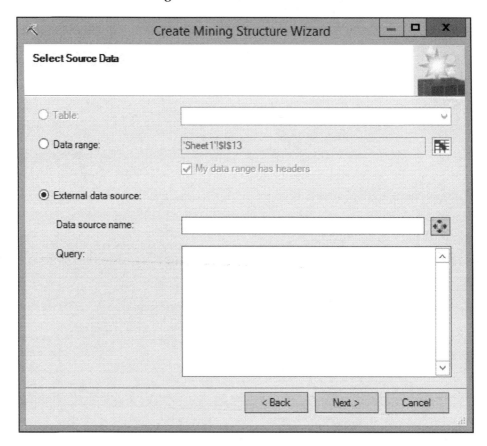

5. Click on the icon next to data source and you will get the **Data Source Query** editor. Then, click on the data source icon again. It will create a new Analysis Services data source, as shown here:

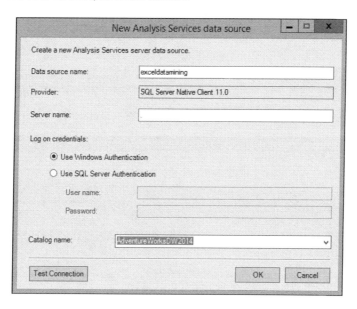

6. Click on **OK** and then select the view **vTargetMail (dbo)**, which we used for our earlier analysis. Finally, click on **OK**, as shown here:

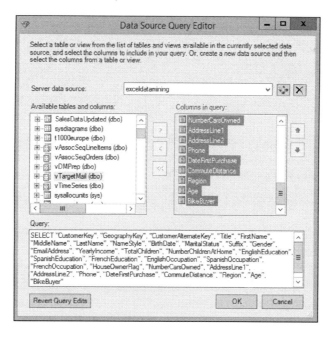

7. The screen returns back to the wizard and shows us the query that we selected. Click on **Next** to go to the screen that allows you to choose the columns and the type, as shown in the following screenshot:

8. Click on **Next** and proceed to the next page that allows you to select the percentage of data and maximum number of rows for testing.

   To understand the importance of setting some data aside for testing, it is important to understand training and testing of the model at this point. Training a model essentially means populating the model with the data and analyzing the content to form nodes of the model. The testing phase involves taking the patterns learned in the training phase and measuring their performance on data that was set aside just prior to training the model.

9. Proceed to the next screen, provide a name to the structure, and then click on **Finish**. We name the example here as `exceldataminingstructure`. We then add a model to the structure by choosing the **Add Model to Structure** option in the **Advanced** tab.

10. The first two screens can be passed through by clicking on the **Next** button. We then select the **Microsoft Decision Trees** algorithm from the **Select Mining Algorithm** screen. The name of the algorithm that will be used to find patterns in the data is Decision Tree (check throughout whether Tree or Trees - Tree in previous chapter).

11. We will now select the columns and their usage, namely, **Input, Predict only**, and so on.

12. Let's work towards a business problem to determine the potential customers of bikes to whom we must send promotional e-mails. Thus, we will change the **BikeBuyer** column to **Input and Predict** or **Predict**, and we will set all the other columns to **Input**, as shown in the following screenshot:

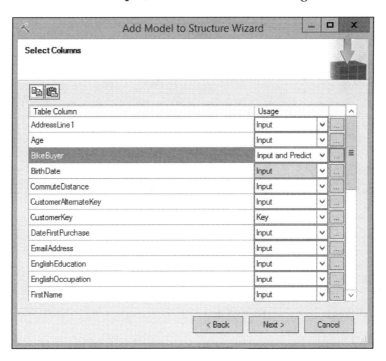

13. The next screen will prompt us to enter **Model name**. Name the model `exceldatamining_DecisionTrees` and leave **Model description** as default, as shown here:

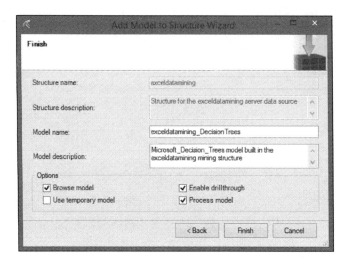

14. Enabling the **Use temporary model** option will create the model, but will not save it to the server; the model will be deleted when the session of Excel is closed. We click on **Finish** to generate the model. We will then get the **Decision Tree** and the **Dependency Network** graphs in two separate tabs, as shown here:

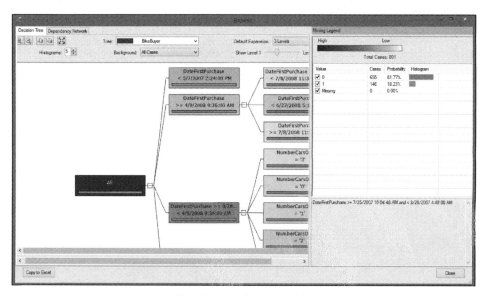

Decision Tree for the Model

As we can see, the probability of a person buying a bike is very closely related to `DateFirstPurchase` and customers with `DateFirstPurchase` less than 5/7/2007 are more likely to buy a bike. The dependency network shows that the `BikeBuyer` parameter is directly related to all the input parameters, as shown in the following screenshot:

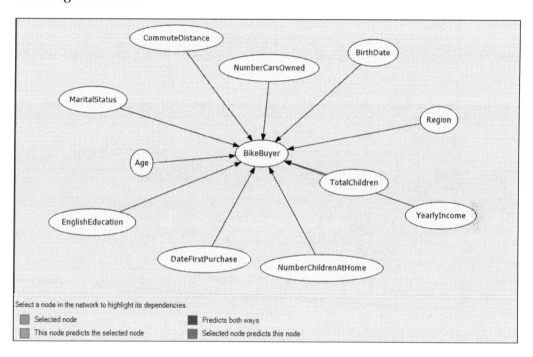

Now that we created and deployed the model, we can execute a simple prediction query against it. We will look for a list of customers and their probability of buying a bike. For this, we will use the **Query** tool in the **DATA MINING** tab, as shown in the following screenshot:

Location of the Query tool in the Data Mining tab

We skip the first three screens of the wizard by clicking on **Next** and then reach the **Choose Output** screen, as shown here:

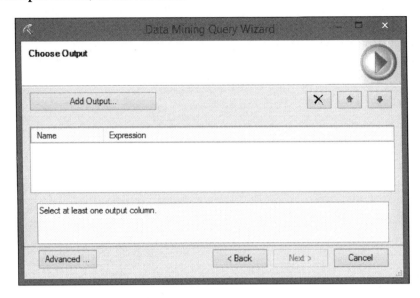

In the preceding screenshot, there are two buttons, namely, **Add Output** and **Advanced**; we will visit each one of them in turn. Click on **Add Output** and then add the two outputs, as shown in the following screenshot:

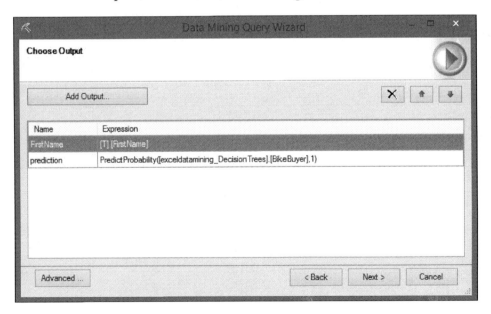

Here, we are using the `PredictProbability` function. The next screen gives us the option to choose the destination for the query results. Choose the new worksheet and then click on **Next** again. The following screenshot shows a small section of the result that will be displayed on a new worksheet:

FirstName	prediction
Diana	0.999302285
Marc	0.999302285
Jesse	0.231648138
Amanda	0.99973549
Megan	0.99973549
Nathan	0.231648138
Adam	0.999302285
Leonard	0.231648138
Christine	0.999302285
Jaclyn	0.999302285
Jeremy	0.999302285
Carol	0.231648138
Alan	0.999302285
Daniel	6.19E-05
Heidi	0.999302285
Ana	0.99973549
Deanna	0.999302285
Gilbert	0.999302285
Michele	0.999302285
Carl	0.999302285
Marc	0.999302285
Ashlee	0.157280175
Jon	0.999302285
Todd	0.999302285
Noah	0.99973549

The Excel data mining add-in also provides us with the ability to validate and test the models that we create. We have the option to create an **Accuracy Chart**, a **Classification Matrix**, a **Profit Chart**, and a **Cross-Validation** of models; these options are present in the **Accuracy and Validation** section, as shown in the following screenshot:

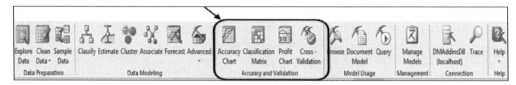

Location of the Accuracy and Validation Section on the excel menu ribbon

Let's modify the query and get the value of the name of the customer, the yearly income, and the number of children in the query along with the predicted probability. We will now perform the what-if scenario analysis and see the effect of changing the values of a few attributes on the predictable or other attributes. When the result is displayed on the worksheet, the **TABLE TOOLS** tab with **ANALYZE** option is automatically highlighted, as shown in the following screenshot:

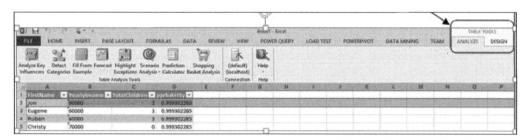

Table Tools has two sub tabs: Analyze and Design

Choose the **Scenario Analysis** option and then **What-If** to perform the what-if analysis. We will be presented with the following dialog box:

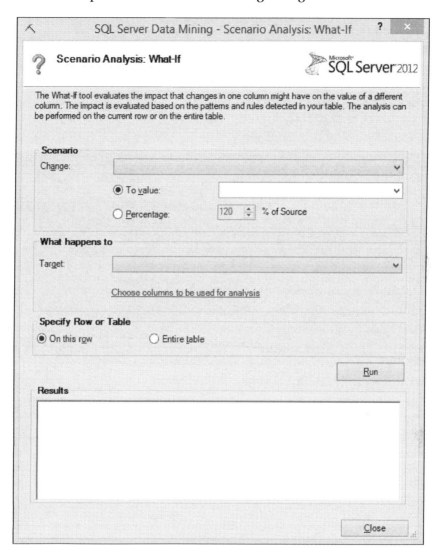

Choose the row with the following attributes value for our what-if analysis:

- **Name:** Jon
- **YearlyIncome:** 90000
- **TotalChildren:** 2
- **Probability:** 0.999302285

Let's now try to predict the probability if the value of the total number of children is changed to 3. Enter the data into the **Change** and **Target** section, as shown in the following screenshot and then click on **Run:**

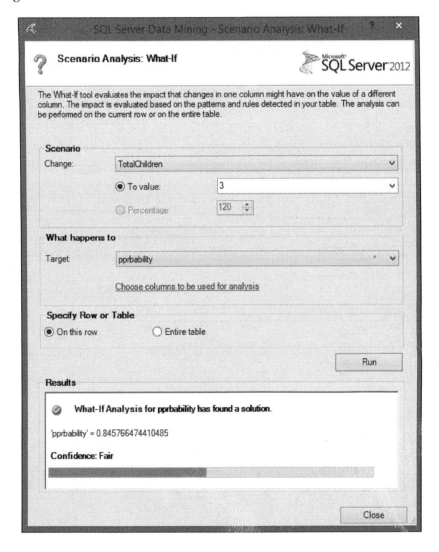

Now, we can see that there is a drop from **0.99** to **0.84** in the customer's probability of buying the bike if there is a change in the number of children in his/her family. Until now, we discussed a few features that are available once we install the data mining add-in. The article at `http://msdn.microsoft.com/en-us/library/dn282385.aspx` discusses all the features that are enabled once we install the data mining add-in for Excel.

Data mining using HDInsight and Microsoft Azure Machine Learning

As mentioned earlier, it is not uncommon to be in a situation wherein the data is not only huge in volume, but also rich in variety. In such a scenario, we will need to employ the Big Data solution, which is popularly known as Hadoop, to perform the data handling tasks. The link at `http://hadooptutorial.wikispaces.com/Hadoop+architecture` provides a brief overview of the Hadoop architecture. As it is impossible to transfer such huge volumes of data across systems, it becomes a necessity to have the data mining functionality either built-in or provided by some additional project in the form of an add-in. These add-ins are often open source projects and hosted on the Apache Software Foundation website. The project that provides us with this capability is known as Mahout. HDInsight is the Big Data solution provided by Microsoft as a service on Azure. **Microsoft Azure Machine Learning (MAML)** is another solution on Azure that has seamless integration with HDInsight. It provides an excellent Machine Learning Driven Data Mining capability as a service on Azure.

To use Mahout, we will need to download the latest Mahout JAR file from the Apache site at `http://mahout.apache.org/`. Mahout is a continuously developing project and we can expect new algorithms and new capabilities being continuously added to it. The latest list of algorithms that is supported by Mahout is available on the Apache site at `http://mahout.apache.org/users/basics/algorithms.html`. For our example, in this chapter, we need to use HDInsight PowerShell cmdlets. A complete list of HDInsight PowerShell cmdlets can be found at `http://msdn.microsoft.com/en-us/library/dn479228.aspx`. We will also need an HDInsight cluster configured for us to use Mahout. At the time of writing this book, Mahout is not supported by Microsoft. However, it can be used on the Microsoft Azure Platform.

It is worthwhile to have a small tour of the Microsoft Azure Management Portal so that you have more clarity on the next example.

Microsoft Azure

Microsoft Azure is the cloud computing platform provided by Microsoft that offers a set of services, APIs, and tools and technologies that allow you to model an unlimited number of scenarios built in the cloud. The URL for the Microsoft Azure Management portal is `https://manage.windowsazure.com`. To begin using the Azure services, we need to have the Azure subscription enabled. The article at `http://azure.microsoft.com/en-us/pricing/purchase-options/` lists the different purchase options available to avail Azure services. Once logged in, we can have a glimpse of the services that we can configure on Azure and also configure more services if we wish to. The following screenshot shows the Microsoft Azure Management portal:

The all items interface on Azure

The column on the left-hand side gives us information about the services available, while the services configured are listed on the right-hand side of the screen. We will take a tour of Microsoft HDInsight and Microsoft Azure Machine Learning, and then see how to use their power to get some predictions for our business problems.

Microsoft HDInsight

Microsoft HDInsight is another service available in Microsoft Azure; we can get to the management portal of an HDInsight cluster by clicking on the HDInsight link on the portal. This will open the following HDInsight page:

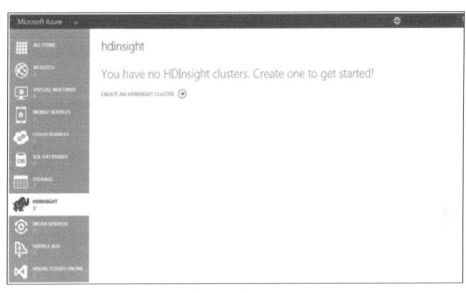

Azure HDInsight Service Portal

HDInsight PowerShell

At the beginning of this chapter, we referred to a link that discussed the architecture of Hadoop. We will build on that to discuss the HDInsight PowerShell cmdlets, which provides the user with an easy and convenient way to create, manage, and submit jobs to an HDInsight cluster and get the results of the job execution back to the client. We will now go through setting up PowerShell on a client machine, connect to the subscription, submit the job to the cluster, and get the result. We will now configure PowerShell for HDInsight and then submit the Mahout jobs on a sample data. We will follow the `http://azure.microsoft.com/en-us/documentation/articles/install-configure-powershell/` link to configure the Azure PowerShell and connect to the subscription. We will also install the HDInsight PowerShell tools from `http://azure.microsoft.com/en-us/documentation/articles/install-configure-powershell/#Install`. Once we have installed Windows Azure PowerShell, we can do a quick check, using the following command, whether the required module is loaded or not:

```
Get-Command *HDInsight*
```

If the modules are loaded properly, we will get the following listing:

```
PS C:\Users\amarpb> Get-Command   *HDInsight*

CommandType      Name                                              ModuleName
-----------      ----                                              ----------
Alias            Add-AzureHDInsightConfigValues                    Azure
Alias            Add-AzureHDInsightMetastore                       Azure
Alias            Add-AzureHDInsightStorage                         Azure
Alias            Get-AzureHDInsightCluster                         Azure
Alias            Get-AzureHDInsightJob                             Azure
Alias            Get-AzureHDInsightJobOutput                       Azure
Alias            Get-AzureHDInsightProperties                      Azure
Alias            New-AzureHDInsightCluster                         Azure
Alias            New-AzureHDInsightClusterConfig                   Azure
Alias            New-AzureHDInsightHiveJobDefinition               Azure
Alias            New-AzureHDInsightMapReduceJobDefinition          Azure
Alias            New-AzureHDInsightPigJobDefinition                Azure
Alias            New-AzureHDInsightSqoopJobDefinition              Azure
Alias            New-AzureHDInsightStreamingMapReduceJobDefinition Azure
Alias            Remove-AzureHDInsightCluster                      Azure
Alias            Revoke-AzureHDInsightHttpServicesAccess           Azure
Alias            Set-AzureHDInsightDefaultStorage                  Azure
Alias            Start-AzureHDInsightJob                           Azure
Alias            Stop-AzureHDInsightJob                            Azure
Alias            Use-AzureHDInsightCluster                         Azure
Alias            Wait-AzureHDInsightJob                            Azure
Cmdlet           Grant-AzureHDInsightHttpServicesAccess            Azure
Cmdlet           Invoke-AzureHDInsightHiveJob                      Azure
```

We will now configure our subscription to be used by installing the certificate in our local machines using the following command:

```
Get-AzurePublishSettingsFile
```

This command will download the publishsettings file, and we will be redirected to the login page on Microsoft Azure. After we successfully log in, we will be able to download the publishsettings file. The structure of the publishsettings file is as follows:

```
<?xml version="1.0" encoding="utf-8"?>
<PublishData>
  <PublishProfile
    SchemaVersion="2.0"
    PublishMethod="AzureServiceManagementAPI">
    <Subscription
      ServiceManagementUrl="https://management.core.windows.net"
      Id="…."
      Name="…"
      ManagementCertificate="…" />
  </PublishProfile>
</PublishData>
```

Here, I have included ... in place of the information that is prepopulated in the `publishsettings` file. We need to import the certificate to the client machine, which can be done using the following command:

`Import-AzurePublishSettingsFile`

We will return to the command prompt if the import of the certificate is successful. To determine whether the certificate is installed properly, we can type the following command-line interface:

`Get-AzureSubscription`

We will get the information about the certificate as follows:

```
SubscriptionName                           : subscription name
SubscriptionId                             : subscription id
ServiceEndpoint                            endpoint
ResourceManagerEndpoint                    :
GalleryEndpoint                            :
ActiveDirectoryEndpoint                    :
ActiveDirectoryTenantId                    :
ActiveDirectoryServiceEndpointResourceId   :
SqlDatabaseDnsSuffix                       : dnssuffix
IsDefault                                  : True
Certificate                                : certificate
CurrentStorageAccountName                  :
ActiveDirectoryUserId                      :
TokenProvider                              : token
```

We will now try to execute the example that is elaborated at `https://mahout.apache.org/users/classification/partial-implementation.html`, which is based on the Classification algorithm as discussed in *Chapter 5, Classification Models*, and we will get the same result on HDInsight.

We will download the required files from `http://nsl.cs.unb.ca/NSL-KDD/` and download the full training set from `http://nsl.cs.unb.ca/NSL-KDD/KDDTrain+.arff`.

We will now copy the Mahout JAR file and sample files to HDInsight Windows Azure Storage Blob (that is what the Azure Blob storage for HDInsight is called), as shown in the following command:

```
$subscriptionName = "<subscription name for HDInsight cluster>"

$storageAccountName = "<storage account for HDinsight cluster>"

$containerName = "<containername for HDInsight cluster>"

$fileName ="<Location\FileName on local machine>"

# Uploading file under the folder mahout

$blobName = "mahout/<FileName>"

Select-AzureSubscription $subscriptionName

$storageaccountkey = get-azurestoragekey $storageAccountName |
%{$_.Primary}

# Create the storage context object

$destContext = New-AzureStorageContext -StorageAccountName
$storageAccountName -StorageAccountKey $storageaccountkey

# Copy the file from local workstation to the Blob
container

Set-AzureStorageBlobContent -File $filename -Container
$containerName -Blob $blobName -context $destContext
```

With HDInsight 3.1, Mahout is available natively in the HDInsight cluster. Install Mahout at the C:\apps\dist\mahout-0.9.0.2.1.3.0-1887 location.

We will now upload the data file for our classification model. Copy the data from http://nsl.cs.unb.ca/NSL-KDD/KDDTrain+.arff to a file named KDDTrain+. arff and the data from http://nsl.cs.unb.ca/NSL-KDD/KDDTest+.arff to a file named KDDTest+.arff.

When we upload the files, we will see the following file listing:

Listing of the files on Windows Azure Blob Storage

The basics of PowerShell, which we discussed, can be helpful to us while working with Mahout on the previous versions of HDInsight. However, since the default version is always going to be the latest version and we have the Mahout command-line utility present, it is just a matter of time that we will have the PowerShell add-in available.

We will remote to the name node of the HDInsight cluster and then create the descriptor file, as shown at `https://mahout.apache.org/users/classification/partial-implementation.html` using the following command on the Hadoop command-line interface:

```
Mahout org.apache.mahout.classifier.df.tools.Describe
-p /mahout/KDDTrain+.arff
-f /mahout/KDDTrain+.info
-d N 3 C 2 N C 4 N C 8 N 2 C 19 N L
```

The output of the preceding command is as follows:

Successful execution of the command

We now have the `.info` file with us in the `/mahout` folder and can be listed by passing the following command in the Hadoop command-line interface:

```
Hadoop fs -ls /mahout
```

The output is shown in the following screenshot:

```
C:\apps\dist\mahout-0.9.0.2.1.3.0-1887\bin>hadoop fs -ls /mahout
Found 3 items
-rwxrwxrwx   1                  3388428 2014-07-05 18:52 /mahout/KDDTest+.arff
-rwxrwxrwx   1                 18868277 2014-07-05 18:53 /mahout/KDDTrain+.arff
-rw-r--r--   1 amar supergroup     2795 2014-07-05 18:58 /mahout/KDDTrain+.info
```

Listing of the files after execution of the command

We will now execute the example to build the classification forest. The command given on the website is as follows:

```
$MAHOUT_HOME/examples/target/mahout-examples--job.jar
org.apache.mahout.classifier.df.mapreduce.BuildForest -
Dmapred.max.split.size=1874231 -d testdata/KDDTrain+.arff -ds
testdata/KDDTrain+.info -sl 5 -p -t 100 -o nsl-forest
```

We will use a modified version of the preceding query as follows:

```
mahout org.apache.mahout.classifier.df.mapreduce.BuildForest -d
testdata/KDDTrain+.arff -ds testdata/KDDTrain+.info -sl 5 -p -t 100 -
o nsl-forest
```

The resultant model is generated in the `/user/<username>/nsl-forest` folder. It can be listed by typing the following command:

```
Hadoop fs -ls /user/<username>/nsl-forest
```

We will copy this folder to the /mahout folder where we have the Train and Test files present using the Hadoop fs -cp command, as follows:

```
Hadoop fs -cp /user/<username>/nsl-forest /mahout
```

We will now use the generated forest file to classify a new data and try to interpret the results. For this, we will use the following command:

```
Mahout org.apache.mahout.classifier.df.mapreduce.TestForest -i
/mahout/KDDTest+.arff -ds /mahout/KDDTrain+.info -m /mahout/nsl-
forest -a -mr -o predictions
```

The output of the preceding command is as follows:

```
C:\apps\dist\mahout-0.9.0.2.1.3.0-1887\bin>mahout org.apache.mahout.
classifier.df.mapreduce.TestForest -i /mahout/KDDTest+.arff -ds /mahout/
KDDTrain+.info -m /maho

/nsl-forest -a -mr -o predictions

"Mahout home set C:\apps\dist\mahout-0.9.0.2.1.3.0-1887"

"MAHOUT_LOCAL is not set; adding HADOOP_CONF_DIR to classpath."

MAHOUT_JOB: C:\apps\dist\mahout-0.9.0.2.1.3.0-1887\examples\target\
mahout-examples-0.9.0.2.1.3.0-1887-job.jar

14/07/06 05:18:48 WARN driver.MahoutDriver: No org.apache.mahout.
classifier.df.mapreduce.TestForest.props found
on classpath, will use command-line arguments only

14/07/06 05:18:50 INFO mapreduce.Classifier: Adding the dataset to
the DistributedCache

14/07/06 05:18:50 INFO mapreduce.Classifier: Adding the decision
forest to the DistributedCache

14/07/06 05:18:50 INFO mapreduce.Classifier: Configuring the
job...

14/07/06 05:18:50 INFO mapreduce.Classifier: Running the job...

14/07/06 05:18:50 INFO client.RMProxy: Connecting to ResourceManager at
headnodehost/100.71.158.25:9010

14/07/06 05:18:52 INFO input.FileInputFormat: Total input paths to
process : 1

14/07/06 05:18:53 INFO mapreduce.JobSubmitter: number of splits:1

14/07/06 05:18:53 INFO mapreduce.JobSubmitter: Submitting tokens
for job: job_1404582766209_0002

14/07/06 05:18:54 INFO impl.YarnClientImpl: Submitted application
application_1404582766209_0002

14/07/06 05:18:54 INFO mapreduce.Job: The url to track the job:
http://headnodehost:9014/proxy/application_1404582766209_0002/
```

```
14/07/06 05:18:54 INFO mapreduce.Job: Running job: job_1404582766209_0002

14/07/06 05:19:06 INFO mapreduce.Job: Job job_1404582766209_0002
running in uber mode : false

14/07/06 05:19:06 INFO mapreduce.Job:  map 0% reduce 0%

14/07/06 05:19:21 INFO mapreduce.Job:  map 100% reduce 0%

14/07/06 05:19:22 INFO mapreduce.Job: Job job_1404582766209_0002
completed successfully

14/07/06 05:19:23 INFO mapreduce.Job: Counters: 30
        File System Counters
                FILE: Number of bytes read=2539347
                FILE: Number of bytes written=100121
                FILE: Number of read operations=0
                FILE: Number of large read operations=0
                FILE: Number of write operations=0
                WASB: Number of bytes read=3388558
                WASB: Number of bytes written=455498
                WASB: Number of read operations=0
                WASB: Number of large read operations=0
                WASB: Number of write operations=0
        Job Counters
                Launched map tasks=1
                Other local map tasks=1
                Total time spent by all maps in occupied slots
(ms)=12005
                Total time spent by all reduces in occupied slots
(ms)=0
                Total time spent by all map tasks (ms)=12005
                Total vcore-seconds taken by all map tasks=12005
                Total megabyte-seconds taken by all map
tasks=12293120
        Map-Reduce Framework
                Map input records=22544
                Map output records=22545
                Input split bytes=132
                Spilled Records=0
                Failed Shuffles=0
                Merged Map outputs=0
```

```
              GC time elapsed (ms)=79

              CPU time spent (ms)=4562

              Physical memory (bytes) snapshot=214188032

              Virtual memory (bytes) snapshot=446746624

              Total committed heap usage (bytes)=202375168

      File Input Format Counters

              Bytes Read=3388426

      File Output Format Counters

              Bytes Written=455498
14/07/06 05:19:24 INFO common.HadoopUtil: Deleting
predictions/mappers

14/07/06 05:19:24 INFO mapreduce.TestForest:

=========================================================
Summary

---------------------------------------------------------
Correctly Classified Instances:      17786      78.8946%
Incorrectly Classified Instances:     4758      21.1054%
Total Classified Instances     :      22544


=========================================================
Confusion Matrix

---------------------------------------------------------

a       b          <--Classified as
9439    272      |  9711        a    = normal
4486    8347     |  12833       b    = anomaly


=========================================================
Statistics

---------------------------------------------------------
Kappa                                  0.5911
Accuracy                               78.8946%
Reliability                            54.0808%
Reliability (standard deviation)        0.4952


14/07/06 05:19:24 INFO driver.MahoutDriver: Program took 36284 ms
(Minutes: 0.6047333333333333)
```

We can get the matrix such as reliability, kappa, accuracy, and the instances that have been correctly classified from the preceding table. This algorithm is still being worked on. The article at `http://azure.microsoft.com/en-us/documentation/articles/hdinsight-mahout/` provides more information about Mahout on HDInsight.

Microsoft Azure Machine Learning

Microsoft Azure Machine Learning provides the data mining capability combined with the unsupervised capability of the Machine Learning algorithm in a very simple and easy-to-use service on Azure. The interaction with Machine Learning is two phase. The first phase is popularly called as the experiment phase; in this phase, we start with the data and clean it up, input the cleaned data into the model, train the model, and then validate the model. The second phase is where we put the model behind a web service and make it available to be used.

The Azure Management portal for Machine Learning is shown in the following screenshot:

Azure Management Portal

We will create a workspace by clicking on the arrow next to **CREATE AN ML WORKSPACE** option, as seen in the preceding screenshot. This will bring up a create workspace screen. We will provide the required input and click on the **CREATE AN ML WORKSPACE**, as shown in the following screenshot:

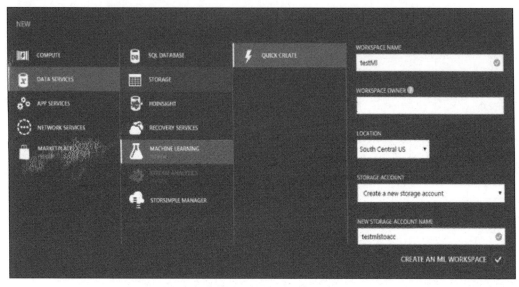

ML Workspace creation wizard

Once the workspace is created, we can see it listed in the Azure portal. We can click on the workspace and navigate to the dashboard, as shown here:

ML Dashboard

Clicking on the **Sign-in to ML Studio** option will open the login page and after a successful login, we will be redirected to the following **ML Studio** page:

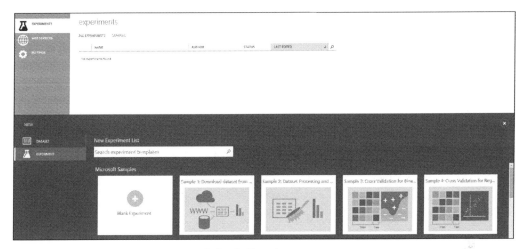

ML Studio Experiments page

We will now follow the step-by-step procedure mentioned in the article at `http://azure.microsoft.com/en-us/documentation/articles/machine-learning-create-experiment/` to create a simple experiment in Azure Machine Learning Studio. The article at `azure.microsoft.com/en-us/documentation/services/machine-learning/tutorials/` provides us with Machine Learning tutorials and guides us to work and interact with Microsoft Azure Machine Learning.

Summary

In this chapter, we discussed data mining using the Excel plugin and HDInsight, Microsoft's Big Data platform on Azure. We also discussed how to get started with Microsoft Azure Machine Learning. Having an idea about other Microsoft products that provide us with the data mining capabilities is beneficial as we can then compare and employ the data mining solution and employ the best-fitting platform for the business and its people.

We will be working with a practical scenario and try to tune the algorithms in the next chapter.

9
Tuning the Models

In the previous chapters, we looked at how we can use different algorithms to perform a number of data mining tasks to get the information we are looking for. Now, it's time to put all the knowledge that we have gathered to practical implementation and see how accurately we can predict the results. We will use real-world data and predict the results that will be of importance. We will also frame the problem statement and then apply data mining algorithms to get the prediction for the problem statement.

Getting the real-world data

There are many publicly available datasets that we can download and extract information from, determine some trends, and so on. We will use the **Housing Affordability Data System (HADS)** dataset to get a sneak peek into the average housing conditions in 2011. The data contains details such as affordability, income, fair market rent, and so on, which will be particularly helpful to derive a few deep observations.

We can download the data from `http://www.huduser.org/portal/datasets/` `hads/hads2011(ASCII).zip`. There is only one file in the dataset, named `thads2011.txt`. We will create a database in the SQL Server instance of the name `HousingAffordabilityData` and import this file into the database with the table name `thads2011`. We will have to import the file as a flat file source into the SQL table. The following screenshot shows a portion of the data in a few columns:

Sample portion of the HADS data imported into SQL Server

Although we used only one year's data, that is, belonging to the year 2011, we have 145,531 rows of data; we can split the data into training and testing with plenty of data to be a part of training and testing. We can similarly collect the data for other years too, but for now, let's derive information from this data for this exercise.

Building the decision tree model

Now that we have obtained quite a large amount of data, we will understand the pattern of correlation between the houses built and the population that occupies these houses. We will look for the patterns, such as the year in which these houses were built, how many bedrooms they have, whether they are rented out, what is the total salary of the people who live in a particular region, and so on. The Microsoft Classification algorithm will help us in these endeavors, and we will also use the Microsoft decision tree. We will use the CONTROL column as the key column and choose AGE1, BEDRMS, FMR, OWNRENT, PER, REGION, TENURE, TOTSAL, UTILITY, ROOMS, and BUILT for the predictable columns and similar ones to be the input columns too. The document at `http://www.` `huduser.org/portal/datasets/hads/HADS_doc.pdf` explains all the fields in detail. Let's elaborate the fields that we are using for our model:

- CONTROL: This is the AHS control number
- AGE1: This is the age of the householder
- BEDRMS: This is the number of bedrooms in a unit
- FMR: This is the fair market rent
- OWNRENT: This is the tenure (house either owned, vacant, or rented)
- PER: These are the number of persons in the household
- REGION: This is the number that depicts one of the four census regions
- TENURE: This is the owner or renter

- TOTSAL: This is the total salary of all the members in a household
- UTILITY: This is the utility cost associated with each house
- ROOMS: This is the number of rooms in the unit
- BUILT: This is the year in which the unit was built

Using the following query, let's get a listing of the data in the table for these columns:

```
Select
control,age1,bedrms,fmr,ownrent,per,region,tenure,totsal,utility,
rooms,built from [HousingAffordabilityData].[dbo].[thads2011];
```

The following screenshot shows the output of the preceding query:

	control	age1	bedrms	fmr	ownrent	per	region	tenure	totsal	utility	rooms
1	'152000021984'	-9	3	1025	'1'	-6	'3'	'-6'	-9	55.833333333	6
2	'152000021985'	-9	2	811	'2'	-6	'3'	'-6'	-9	181	4
3	'152000021986'	46	2	811	'1'	2	'3'	'1'	110000	167	5
4	'152000021988'	28	3	1025	'1'	4	'3'	'1'	72000	273.66666667	6
5	'152000021989'	-9	3	1025	'2'	-6	'3'	'-6'	-9	224.5	6
6	'152000021990'	67	2	811	'1'	2	'3'	'1'	0	196.83333333	6
7	'152000021991'	35	2	811	'1'	1	'3'	'1'	20000	144	4
8	'152000021993'	30	3	1025	'1'	1	'3'	'1'	22500	149	5
9	'152000021994'	59	4	1190	'1'	2	'3'	'1'	34000	249.33333333	7
10	'152000021995'	87	3	1025	'1'	1	'3'	'1'	0	239	7
11	'152000021996'	53	5	1179	'2'	1	'3'	'2'	60000	217.08333333	8
12	'152000021998'	51	3	1025	'2'	1	'3'	'2'	26000	67	5

Let's check the data types of these columns using the following query:

```
select COLUMN_NAME, DATA_TYPE, CHARACTER_MAXIMUM_LENGTH,
IS_NULLABLE
from INFORMATION_SCHEMA.COLUMNS IC
where TABLE_NAME = 'thads2011' and COLUMN_NAME in
(CONTROL,AGE1,REGION,FMR,PER,BEDRMS,TENURE,ROOMS,OWNRNT,
,UTILITY,TOTSAL);
```

The output for the preceding query is shown in the following screenshot:

	COLUMN_NAME	DATA_TYPE	CHARACTER_MAXIMUM_LENGTH	IS_NULLABLE
1	CONTROL	varchar	50	YES
2	AGE1	varchar	50	YES
3	REGION	varchar	50	YES
4	FMR	varchar	50	YES
5	PER	varchar	50	YES
6	BEDRMS	varchar	50	YES
7	TENURE	varchar	50	YES
8	ROOMS	varchar	50	YES
9	OWNRENT	varchar	50	YES
10	UTILITY	varchar	50	YES
11	TOTSAL	varchar	50	YES

From the preceding two screenshots, we can see that there is a need for data cleansing. We also need to change the data type of the columns so that they represent the values correctly.

We first change the data by removing the leading and trailing quotes from the data of our interest using the following query:

```
update [dbo].[thads2011] set
control= SUBSTRING(CONTROL,2,LEN(control)-2),
ownrent=SUBSTRING(ownrent,2,LEN(ownrent)-2),
region=SUBSTRING(region,2,LEN(region)-2),
tenure=SUBSTRING(tenure,2,LEN(tenure)-2)
from [dbo].[thads2011];
```

We can extend the preceding query to remove the quotations for the data of the other column, but at present, we need not worry about the data. After the preceding query is executed, we once again check the content of the columns, as shown in the following screenshot:

	control	age1	bedrms	fmr	ownrent	per	region	tenure	totsal	utility	rooms
1	152000021984	-9	3	1025	1	-6	3	-6	-9	55.833333333	6
2	152000021985	-9	2	811	2	-6	3	-6	-9	181	4
3	152000021986	46	2	811	1	2	3	1	110000	167	5
4	152000021988	28	3	1025	1	4	3	1	72000	273.66666667	6
5	152000021989	-9	3	1025	2	-6	3	-6	-9	224.5	6
6	152000021990	67	2	811	1	2	3	1	0	196.83333333	6
7	152000021991	35	2	811	1	1	3	1	20000	144	4
8	152000021993	30	3	1025	1	1	3	1	22500	149	5
9	152000021994	59	4	1190	1	2	3	1	34000	249.33333333	7
10	152000021995	87	3	1025	1	1	3	1	0	239	7
11	152000021996	53	5	1179	2	1	3	2	60000	217.08333333	8
12	152000021998	51	3	1025	2	1	3	2	26000	67	5
13	152000021999	48	2	811	1	1	3	1	0	116	5
14	152000022000	46	3	1025	1	3	3	1	90000	187	6
15	152000022002	62	3	1025	1	2	3	1	0	284	7

Now, we need to perform the following two data cleansing tasks:

- Correct the data type of the columns under consideration
- Remove the negative and absurd values, for instance, having -9 as the age does not make any sense

For the first task, we have to create a new table and transfer the data to a new table from an old table. The new table that we named thads2011_datatypecorrected is created with the help of the following query:

```
USE [HousingAffordabilityData]
GO

CREATE TABLE [dbo].[thads2011_datatypecorrected](
    [CONTROL] bigint,
    [AGE1] int,
    [METRO3] [varchar](50) ,
    [REGION] int,
    [LMED] [varchar](50) ,
    [FMR] int,
```

```
[L30] [varchar](50),
[L50] [varchar](50) ,
[L80] [varchar](50) ,
[IPOV] [varchar](50) ,
[PER] int,
[ZINC2] [varchar](50) ,
[ZADEQ] [varchar](50) ,
[ZSMHC] [varchar](50) ,
[STATUS] [varchar](50) ,
[WEIGHT] [varchar](50) ,
[BEDRMS] int,
[BUILT] [varchar](50) ,
[TYPE] [varchar](50) ,
[VALUE] [varchar](50) ,
[VACANCY] [varchar](50) ,
[TENURE] int,
[NUNITS] [varchar](50) ,
[ROOMS] int,
[STRUCTURETYPE] [varchar](50) ,
[OWNRENT] int,
[UTILITY] float,
[OTHERCOST] [varchar](50) ,
[COST06] [varchar](50) ,
[COST12] [varchar](50) ,
[COST08] [varchar](50) ,
[COSTMED] [varchar](50) ,
[TOTSAL] int ,
[ASSISTED] [varchar](50) ,
[GLMED] [varchar](50) ,
[GL30] [varchar](50) ,
[GL50] [varchar](50) ,
[GL80] [varchar](50) ,
[APLMED] [varchar](50) ,
[ABL30] [varchar](50) ,
[ABL50] [varchar](50) ,
[ABL80] [varchar](50) ,
[ABLMED] [varchar](50) ,
[BURDEN] [varchar](50) ,
[INCRELAMIPCT] [varchar](50) ,
[INCRELAMICAT] [varchar](50) ,
[INCRELPOVPCT] [varchar](50) ,
[INCRELPOVCAT] [varchar](50) ,
[INCRELFMRPCT] [varchar](50) ,
[INCRELFMRCAT] [varchar](50) ,
```

```
[COST06RELAMIPCT]  [varchar](50) ,
[COST06RELAMICAT]  [varchar](50) ,
[COST06RELPOVPCT]  [varchar](50) ,
[COST06RELPOVCAT]  [varchar](50) ,
[COST06RELFMRPCT]  [varchar](50) ,
[COST06RELFMRCAT]  [varchar](50) ,
[COST08RELAMIPCT]  [varchar](50) ,
[COST08RELAMICAT]  [varchar](50) ,
[COST08RELPOVPCT]  [varchar](50) ,
[COST08RELPOVCAT]  [varchar](50) ,
[COST08RELFMRPCT]  [varchar](50) ,
[COST08RELFMRCAT]  [varchar](50) ,
[COST12RELAMIPCT]  [varchar](50) ,
[COST12RELAMICAT]  [varchar](50) ,
[COST12RELPOVPCT]  [varchar](50) ,
[COST12RELPOVCAT]  [varchar](50) ,
[COST12RELFMRPCT]  [varchar](50) ,
[COST12RELFMRCAT]  [varchar](50) ,
[COSTMedRELAMIPCT]  [varchar](50) ,
[COSTMedRELAMICAT]  [varchar](50) ,
[COSTMedRELPOVPCT]  [varchar](50) ,
[COSTMedRELPOVCAT]  [varchar](50) ,
[COSTMedRELFMRPCT]  [varchar](50) ,
[COSTMedRELFMRCAT]  [varchar](50) ,
[FMTZADEQ] [varchar](50) ,
[FMTMETRO3] [varchar](50) ,
[FMTBUILT] [varchar](50) ,
[FMTSTRUCTURETYPE] [varchar](50) ,
[FMTBEDRMS] [varchar](50) ,
[FMTOWNRENT] [varchar](50) ,
[FMTCOST06RELPOVCAT]  [varchar](50) ,
[FMTCOST08RELPOVCAT]  [varchar](50) ,
[FMTCOST12RELPOVCAT]  [varchar](50) ,
[FMTCOSTMEDRELPOVCAT]  [varchar](50) ,
[FMTINCRELPOVCAT]  [varchar](50) ,
[FMTCOST06RELFMRCAT]  [varchar](50) ,
[FMTCOST08RELFMRCAT]  [varchar](50) ,
[FMTCOST12RELFMRCAT]  [varchar](50) ,
[FMTCOSTMEDRELFMRCAT]  [varchar](50) ,
[FMTINCRELFMRCAT]  [varchar](50) ,
[FMTCOST06RELAMICAT]  [varchar](50) ,
[FMTCOST08RELAMICAT]  [varchar](50) ,
[FMTCOST12RELAMICAT]  [varchar](50) ,
[FMTCOSTMEDRELAMICAT]  [varchar](50) ,
```

```
          [FMTINCRELAMICAT]  [varchar](50) ,
          [FMTASSISTED]  [varchar](50) ,
          [FMTBURDEN]  [varchar](50) ,
          [FMTREGION]  [varchar](50) ,
          [FMTSTATUS]  [varchar](50)
     )


     GO
```

We then insert the data into this table from the old table using the following query:

```
     insert into thads2011_datatypecorrected
     select * FROM [HousingAffordabilityData].[dbo].[thads2011];
```

Now that we have the data type as per the requirement, we won't cleanse the data any more. Let's begin by checking how many rows have the value of `age1` that is less than zero. The easiest way to do this is by executing the following query:

```
     select
     control,age1,bedrms,fmr,ownrent,per,region,tenure,totsal,utility,
     rooms from [HousingAffordabilityData].[dbo].[thads2011_
     datatypecorrected]
     where age1<0;
```

We see that there are 10, 613 rows that have the values of `age1`, `per`, `tenure`, and `totsal` less than zero. We can assign a random value to these columns based on the average age, the average number of persons, the tenure, and the total salary of the data that is already present. Since this data accounts for less than 10 percent of the data, we will remove this data from the table using the following query:

```
     delete from
     [HousingAffordabilityData].[dbo].[thads2011_datatypecorrected]
     where age1<0;
```

We will now create the model based on the Decision Tree algorithm; first, name the model `thads2011_decision_trees`. The columns selected for the model and their usage are shown in the following screenshot:

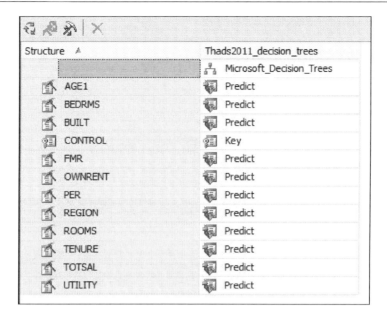

The data mining model in **Mining Model Viewer** for number of bedrooms is shown in the following screenshot:

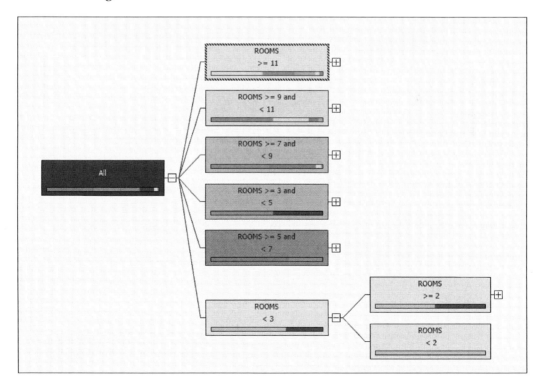

We will now look at the accuracy chart of the model and determine the accuracy of predicting the year in which the unit was built. We provide the prediction year as 2009 and generate a lift chart, as shown in the following screenshot:

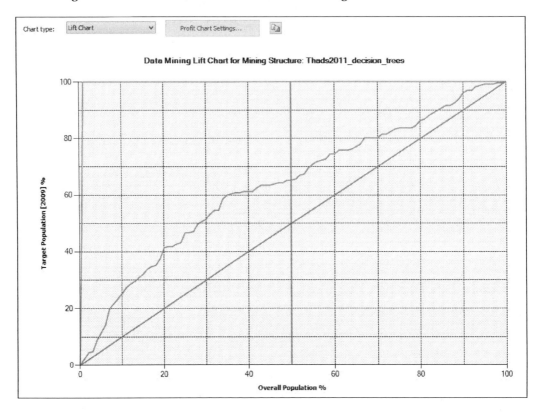

Tuning the model

Let's understand the information conveyed by the lift chart in the preceding screenshot. When a discrete target is selected and target value is specified, a standard lift chart is generated. A standard lift chart always contains a single line for every model that you selected and two additional lines: an ideal line and a random line. The coordinates at each point along the line indicate what percentage of the target audience we can capture if we used this model against the specified percentage of audience.

The top line shows that an ideal model will capture 100 percent of the target using about five percent of the data. This simply implies that five percent of the data indicates the desired target; there is no magic here. The bottom line is the random line. The random line is always a 45-degree line across the chart. This indicates that if you were to randomly guess the result for each case, you will capture 50 percent of the target using 50 percent of the data; again, no magic here. The other lines on the chart represent the data mining model. Hopefully, all the models will be above the random line. When a model's line is hovering around the random guess line, it implies that there wasn't sufficient information in the training data to learn patterns about the target. The data mining legend for the lift chart is shown in the following screenshot:

Mining Legend

Population percentage: 49.50%

Series, Model	Score	Target population	Predict probability
Thads2011_decision_trees	0.64	65.20%	0.51%
Random Guess Model		50.00%	
Ideal Model for: Thads2011_decision_trees		100.00%	

As seen in the preceding screenshot, we have a target population of **65.20%**, which is average. Let's check whether we can make it better. Let's change the score method to 3, which is using the Bayesian with K2 Prior algorithm. The article at `http://msdn.microsoft.com/en-us/library/ms175382.aspx` provides us with more details on the different algorithms for feature selection. The data mining legend with the preceding score method is shown in the following screenshot:

Mining Legend

Population percentage: 49.50%

Series, Model	Score	Target population	Predict probability
Thads2011_decision_trees	0.65	69.16%	0.52%
Random Guess Model		50.00%	
Ideal Model for: Thads2011_decision_trees		100.00%	

We will now change the split method of the tree to 2 using SPLIT_METHOD. This parameter is used to specify the tree shape, for example, whether the tree shape is binary or bushy. The following three methods are used:

- **1**: This indicates that the tree will split only in a binary way, meaning if an attribute **A** has three values (**1**, **2**, and **3**), it can be split into **3** and **not 3**

- **2**: This indicates that the tree should always split completely on each attribute value; in the case of an attribute **A**, it will split into three branches, namely, **1**, **2**, and **3**

- **3**: This indicates that the splitting of the tree will be decided by the Analysis Services to produce the best results

The lift chart legend is shown in the following screenshot:

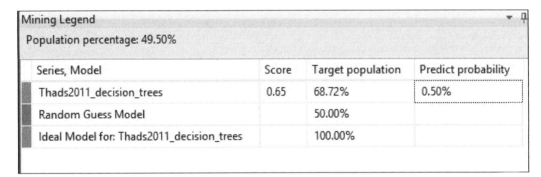

Series, Model	Score	Target population	Predict probability
Thads2011_decision_trees	0.65	68.72%	0.50%
Random Guess Model		50.00%	
Ideal Model for: Thads2011_decision_trees		100.00%	

Mining Legend
Population percentage: 49.50%

Adding a clustering model to the data mining structure

Let's add the clustering model and name it thads2011_clustering_model to this structure and compare the accuracy of the two models. The lift chart with the two models is shown in the following screenshot:

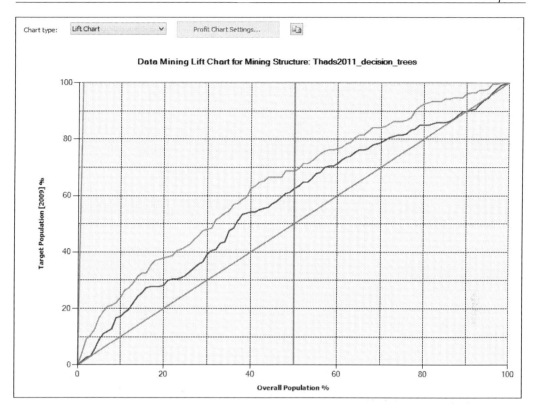

The data mining legend for the two models is shown in the following screenshot:

Mining Legend

Population percentage: 49.50%

Series, Model	Score	Target population	Predict probability
Thads2011_decision_trees	0.65	68.72%	0.50%
thads2011_clustering_model	0.58	62.56%	0.63%
Random Guess Model		50.00%	
Ideal Model for: Thads2011_decision_trees...		100.00%	

From the preceding screenshot, we can see that the lift chart is better for the decision tree than for the clustering model. Let's now change the value of the CLUSTERING METHOD parameter to non-scalable **Expectation Maximization (EM)**. The CLUSTERING METHOD parameter indicates which algorithm is used to determine the cluster membership. By default, the scalable EM method is used, which uses only the first 50,000 records to fit the model. If the model cannot fit using the first 50,000 records, then additional 50,000 records are read. However, in non-scalable EM, the entire dataset is read and it also results in more accurate clusters. The article at http://msdn.microsoft.com/en-us/library/cc280445.aspx gives more information about the Microsoft Clustering algorithm. We reprocess the model and compare the lift chart for the two models again, as shown in the following screenshot:

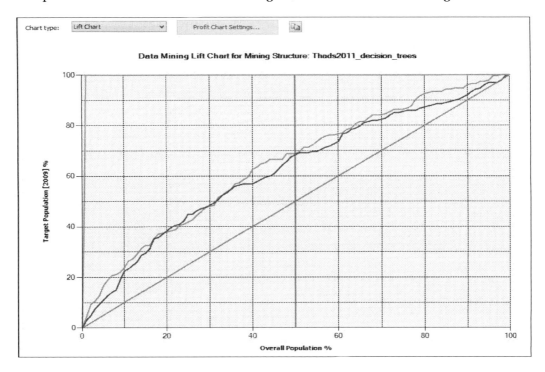

We can see that the lift charts for the two models are now similar. Let's now explore `thads2011_clustering_model` in more detail. We will navigate to the **Cluster diagram** tab and select the value of **Sharing Variable** as **BUILT** and **State** as **2009**, as shown here:

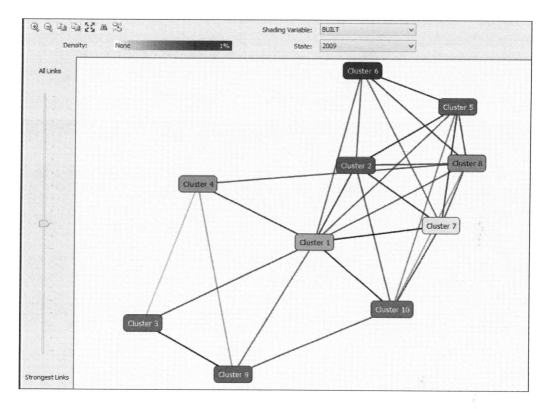

In the preceding screenshot, we can see that **Cluster 6** and **Cluster 5** have the strongest links. The **Cluster Discrimination** tab for the two clusters will give you an idea about the factors that favor one cluster over the other, as shown in the following screenshot:

| Cluster 1: | Cluster 5 | | Cluster 2: | Cluster 6 | |

Discrimination scores for Cluster 5 and Cluster 6

Variables	Values	Favors Cluster 5	Favors Cluster 6
FMR	753 - 1,126	████████	
FMR	1,127 - 3,586		██████████
UTILITY	84.4 - 366.5	█████	
UTILITY	366.5 - 1,341.1		██████
TOTSAL	7,182 - 148,366	███	
ROOMS	5 - 8	███	
ROOMS	9 - 15		████
BEDRMS	3	███	
REGION	3		████
REGION	2	███	
TOTSAL	148,367 - 1,137,526		███
BEDRMS	5		███
TOTSAL	0 - 7,181		▌
BEDRMS	6		▌
PER	1 - 4	▌	
PER	5 - 17		▌
BEDRMS	4		▌
BUILT	1950	▏	
BUILT	1919	▏	

We can choose any cluster for further analysis; it really isn't important which cluster is chosen. One method to pick a cluster is determining which clusters have the strongest links and choose one of them; another method is to pick a cluster that seems far away from the rest. We might have simply found an interesting cluster during our initial exploration. We will usually start by looking at the **Cluster Characteristics** view, which is the third tab in the cluster view that describes the characteristics of the cluster cases by displaying attributes in a decreasing probability.

Adding the Neural Network model to the data mining structure

We will now try to predict the value of some attributes by providing some input values. We will use the Neural Network algorithm and call our model `thads2011_neural_network` for this purpose. The data mining model viewer for the model is shown in the following screenshot:

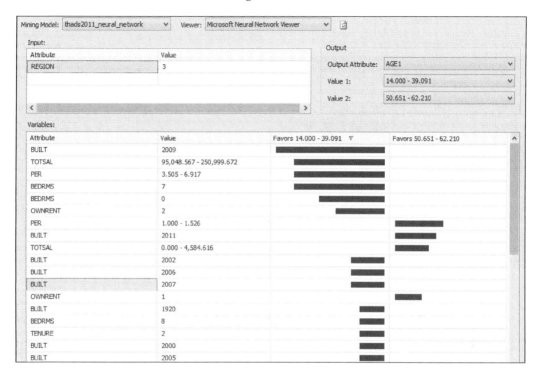

The preceding screenshot shows how different variables favor the range of values of `AGE1` with the input value of the attribute `REGION` as 3. In other words, for region 3, we can see that if a house is built in 2009, then the age of the owner would be in the range of 14 to 39.

Comparing the predictions of different models

We will now try to make some predictions based on the three models that we created earlier. First, we select the decision tree algorithm and then select the case table `thads2011`. We then frame the prediction query, as shown in the following screenshot:

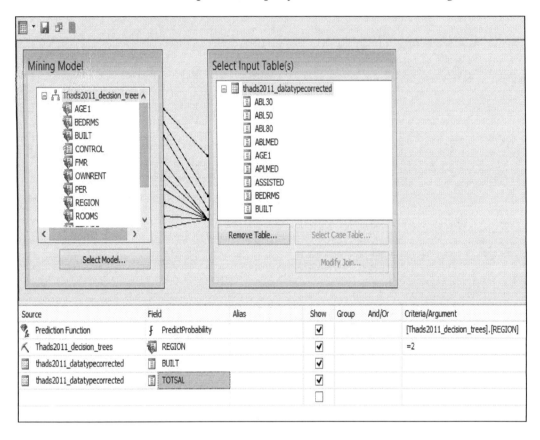

The result of the preceding query is shown in the following screenshot:

Expression	REGION	BUILT	TOTSAL
0.997232472324723	2	1960	32000
0.953551912568306	2	1975	58000
0.997232472324723	2	1975	95000
0.997232472324723	2	1950	48000
0.99403578528827	2	1975	29000
0.997232472324723	2	1950	60000
0.953551912568306	2	1940	0
0.997232472324723	2	1920	14500
0.953551912568306	2	1940	0
0.953551912568306	2	1920	110000
0.997232472324723	2	1950	0
0.953551912568306	2	1995	162000
0.997232472324723	2	1919	0
0.99403578528827	2	2010	10000
0.997232472324723	2	1985	26200
0.997232472324723	2	1950	75000
0.953551912568306	2	1970	25000
0.997232472324723	2	1960	42000
0.99403578528827	2	1960	30000
0.997232472324723	2	1919	64000
0.99403578528827	2	1975	0

From the preceding screenshot, we can make some conclusions about the percentage age probability of two bedrooms in a certain house with certain TOTSAL and BUILT in a certain year. The query used is as follows:

```
SELECT
  PredictProbability([Thads2011_decision_trees].[REGION]),
  [Thads2011_decision_trees].[REGION],
  t.[BUILT],
  t.[TOTSAL]
From
  [Thads2011_decision_trees]
PREDICTION JOIN
```

```
OPENQUERY([Housing Affordability Data],
   'SELECT
      [BUILT],
      [TOTSAL],
      [AGE1],
      [REGION],
      [FMR],
      [PER],
      [BEDRMS],
      [TENURE],
      [ROOMS],
      [OWNRENT],
      [UTILITY]
   FROM
      [dbo].[thads2011_datatypecorrected]
   ') AS t
ON
   [Thads2011_decision_trees].[AGE1] = t.[AGE1] AND
   [Thads2011_decision_trees].[REGION] = t.[REGION] AND
   [Thads2011_decision_trees].[FMR] = t.[FMR] AND
   [Thads2011_decision_trees].[PER] = t.[PER] AND
   [Thads2011_decision_trees].[BEDRMS] = t.[BEDRMS] AND
   [Thads2011_decision_trees].[BUILT] = t.[BUILT] AND
   [Thads2011_decision_trees].[TENURE] = t.[TENURE] AND
   [Thads2011_decision_trees].[ROOMS] = t.[ROOMS] AND
   [Thads2011_decision_trees].[OWNRENT] = t.[OWNRENT] AND
   [Thads2011_decision_trees].[UTILITY] = t.[UTILITY] AND
   [Thads2011_decision_trees].[TOTSAL] = t.[TOTSAL]
WHERE
   [Thads2011_decision_trees].[REGION] =2
```

As it might be evident, we can try different values for different attributes and frame some more prediction queries, which will help us discover some hidden information that might be interesting.

Let's look at the clustering model and try to get the same predictions. We now add the Neural model, as shown in the following screenshot:

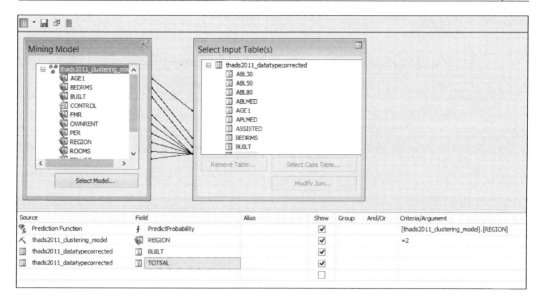

The result of the preceding query is shown in the following screenshot:

Expression	REGION	BUILT	TOTSAL
0.4420537405...	2	2004	110000
0.4512086102...	2	2005	110000
0.5500826576...	2	2007	96000
0.4902860690...	2	2006	9320
0.6141550217...	2	1975	58000
0.4985020420...	2	1975	95000
0.4421015796...	2	1975	29000
0.6647078384...	2	1920	110000
0.5689811993...	2	1995	162000
0.4195041685...	2	2010	10000
0.5531767706...	2	1985	26200
0.4432655491...	2	1970	25000
0.6242341877...	2	1919	64200
0.4423381650...	2	1919	114500
0.5465837229...	2	1970	92000
0.4424089692...	2	1919	70000
0.5875897827...	2	1970	58000
0.6464728346...	2	2004	40000
0.6555093832...	2	2005	120000
0.6525072686...	2	2007	142000
0.5874518133...	2	2008	62000

The query that gets executed is as follows:

```
SELECT
    PredictProbability([thads2011_clustering_model].[REGION]),
    [thads2011_clustering_model].[REGION],
    t.[BUILT],
    t.[TOTSAL]
From
    [thads2011_clustering_model]
PREDICTION JOIN
    OPENQUERY([Housing Affordability Data],
        'SELECT
            [BUILT],
            [TOTSAL],
            [AGE1],
            [REGION],
            [FMR],
            [PER],
            [BEDRMS],
            [TENURE],
            [ROOMS],
            [OWNRENT],
            [UTILITY]
        FROM
            [dbo].[thads2011_datatypecorrected]
        ') AS t
ON
    [thads2011_clustering_model].[AGE1] = t.[AGE1] AND
    [thads2011_clustering_model].[REGION] = t.[REGION] AND
    [thads2011_clustering_model].[FMR] = t.[FMR] AND
    [thads2011_clustering_model].[PER] = t.[PER] AND
    [thads2011_clustering_model].[BEDRMS] = t.[BEDRMS] AND
    [thads2011_clustering_model].[BUILT] = t.[BUILT] AND
    [thads2011_clustering_model].[TENURE] = t.[TENURE] AND
    [thads2011_clustering_model].[ROOMS] = t.[ROOMS] AND
    [thads2011_clustering_model].[OWNRENT] = t.[OWNRENT] AND
    [thads2011_clustering_model].[UTILITY] = t.[UTILITY] AND
    [thads2011_clustering_model].[TOTSAL] = t.[TOTSAL]
WHERE
    [thads2011_clustering_model].[REGION] =2
```

Let's compare the difference in the predictions of the two algorithms by selecting any one of the outputs from the decision tree algorithm. Then, check whether we have the corresponding entry in the clustering model prediction.

We choose the following entry from the decision tree prediction, where the BUILT year is 2009 and TOTSAL is 5400. The query used is as follows:

```
SELECT
  PredictProbability([Thads2011_decision_trees].[REGION]),
  [Thads2011_decision_trees].[REGION],
  t.[BUILT],
  t.[TOTSAL]
From
  [Thads2011_decision_trees]
PREDICTION JOIN
  OPENQUERY([Housing Affordability Data],
    'SELECT
      [BUILT],
      [TOTSAL],
      [AGE1],
      [REGION],
      [FMR],
      [PER],
      [BEDRMS],
      [TENURE],
      [ROOMS],
      [OWNRENT],
      [UTILITY]
    FROM
      [dbo].[thads2011_datatypecorrected]
    ') AS t
ON
  [Thads2011_decision_trees].[AGE1] = t.[AGE1] AND
  [Thads2011_decision_trees].[REGION] = t.[REGION] AND
  [Thads2011_decision_trees].[FMR] = t.[FMR] AND
  [Thads2011_decision_trees].[PER] = t.[PER] AND
  [Thads2011_decision_trees].[BEDRMS] = t.[BEDRMS] AND
  [Thads2011_decision_trees].[BUILT] = t.[BUILT] AND
  [Thads2011_decision_trees].[TENURE] = t.[TENURE] AND
  [Thads2011_decision_trees].[ROOMS] = t.[ROOMS] AND
  [Thads2011_decision_trees].[OWNRENT] = t.[OWNRENT] AND
  [Thads2011_decision_trees].[UTILITY] = t.[UTILITY] AND
  [Thads2011_decision_trees].[TOTSAL] = t.[TOTSAL]
WHERE
  [Thads2011_decision_trees].[REGION] =2 AND
  t.[BUILT] =2008 AND
  t.[TOTSAL] =5400
```

The result of the preceding query is shown in the following screenshot:

Expression	REGION	BUILT	TOTSAL
0.5596330275...	2	2008	5400

Let's modify the query for the clustering model, as follows:

```
SELECT
    PredictProbability([thads2011_clustering_model].[REGION]),
    [thads2011_clustering_model].[REGION],
    t.[TOTSAL],
    t.[BUILT]
From
    [thads2011_clustering_model]
PREDICTION JOIN
    OPENQUERY([Housing Affordability Data],
        'SELECT
            [TOTSAL],
            [BUILT],
            [AGE1],
            [REGION],
            [FMR],
            [PER],
            [BEDRMS],
            [TENURE],
            [ROOMS],
            [OWNRENT],
            [UTILITY]
        FROM
            [dbo].[thads2011_datatypecorrected]
        ') AS t
ON
    [thads2011_clustering_model].[AGE1] = t.[AGE1] AND
    [thads2011_clustering_model].[REGION] = t.[REGION] AND
    [thads2011_clustering_model].[FMR] = t.[FMR] AND
    [thads2011_clustering_model].[PER] = t.[PER] AND
    [thads2011_clustering_model].[BEDRMS] = t.[BEDRMS] AND
    [thads2011_clustering_model].[BUILT] = t.[BUILT] AND
    [thads2011_clustering_model].[TENURE] = t.[TENURE] AND
    [thads2011_clustering_model].[ROOMS] = t.[ROOMS] AND
    [thads2011_clustering_model].[OWNRENT] = t.[OWNRENT] AND
```

```
        [thads2011_clustering_model].[UTILITY] = t.[UTILITY] AND
        [thads2011_clustering_model].[TOTSAL] = t.[TOTSAL]
WHERE
        [thads2011_clustering_model].[REGION] =2 AND
        t.[TOTSAL] =5400 AND
        t.[BUILT] =2008
```

The result of the preceding query is shown in the following screenshot:

Expression	REGION	TOTSAL	BUILT
0.4260689292...	2	5400	2008

As there is not much difference in the score of the two models, we can use either of the two queries. For some of the variables, we see drastic differences in the lift chart of the models. We will tune the models with lower lift chart and then compare the output of the different models.

Let's look at the clustering model and try to get some insights into the data. We frame the query as shown here:

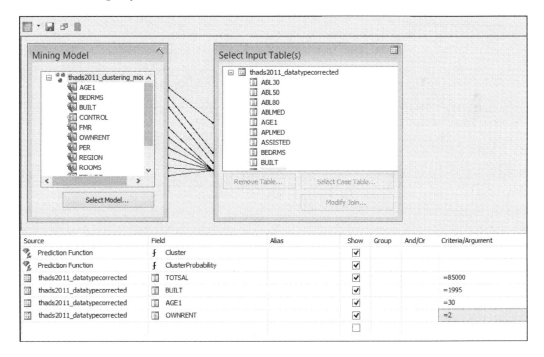

The objective of the preceding query is to determine the cluster to which a data point will belong when TOTSAL is 85000, BUILT is 1995, AGE1 is 30, and OWNRENT is 2. The result of the preceding query is shown in the following screenshot:

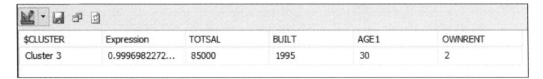

$CLUSTER	Expression	TOTSAL	BUILT	AGE1	OWNRENT
Cluster 3	0.9996982272...	85000	1995	30	2

Summary

In this chapter, we looked at the publicly available datasets and tried to derive some information from them. We tried to alter some parameters to modify the accuracy of the data mining model and then made a few predictions. The chapter puts forth the approach that you should take to perform Data Mining on any dataset that contains information. In the next chapter, we will talk about the problems that users encounter while dealing with data in different stages of Data Mining and look at how we can troubleshoot these problems.

10
Troubleshooting

In the previous chapters, you learned various data mining algorithms and also worked on creating data mining models. While working through various phases of data mining, we faced many problems both conceptually and technically. The following are some of the technical problems that we faced while working our way through this book:

- Only about 4,000 rows get loaded into the SQL table while transferring data from a text file containing 145,000 rows

- Error while changing the data type of the table

- Troubleshooting the data mining models' performance

- Error during the deployment of a model

We will now look at how to resolve each of these problems.

A fraction of rows get transferred into a SQL table

We discussed getting data from `http://www.huduser.org/portal/datasets/hads/hads2011(ASCII).zip` in *Chapter 9*, *Tuning the Models*. This link will provide us with the text file `thads2011.txt`, which is a comma separated file. The different ways in which we can load this text file into the SQL Server are as follows:

- We can change the file extension to `.xls` and then load the data using the Excel provider of the SQL Server Export Import Wizard

- We can use the file as a flat file source and then load the data using the SQL Server Export Import Wizard

- We can use SQL Server integration services to load the data

In the previous chapters, we used the second method because the third method requires us to create a table first and then write a package that will transfer the data from the Excel or CSV file into the SQL table. The first method has an inherent limitation on the number of rows that can be transferred to SQL Server; it is **65535rowstransferred**, as shown in the following screenshot:

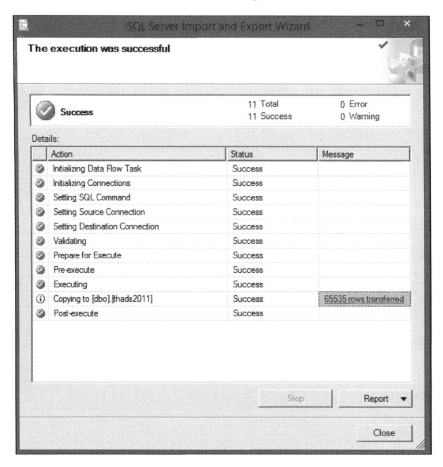

To work around this problem, we can either split the data across multiple worksheets and then load the data into the table, or use the file without any modification to the extensions. We will use **Flat File Source** as shown here:

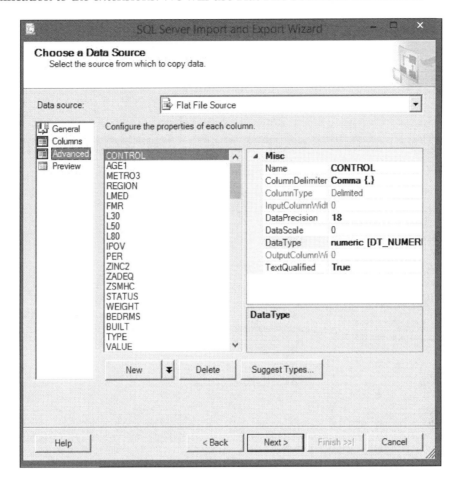

We changed the CONTROL data type to numeric, as shown in the preceding screenshot. On executing the package, we encounter errors, as shown in the following screenshot:

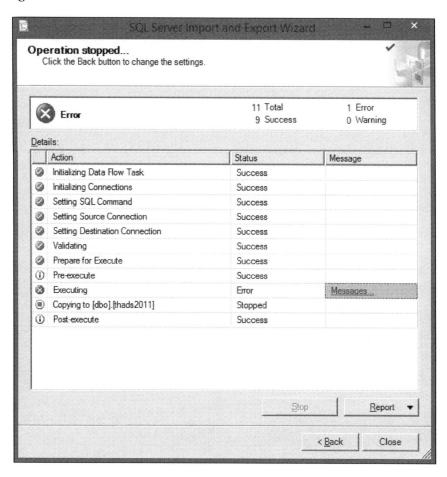

Clicking on the **Messages** link will give us a list of the errors that were encountered during the transfer process, as shown in the following screenshot:

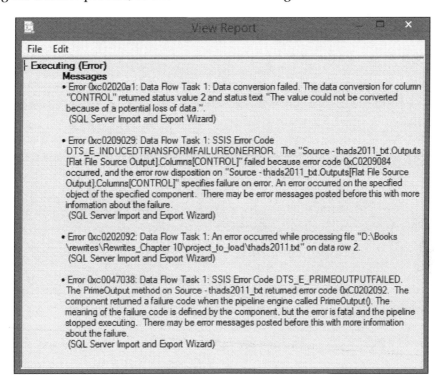

The error message clearly states that the failure is during the conversion of the data type of the CONTROL column. The 036000001146 value is an example of the data in the CONTROL column of the data file. This clearly will not fit into a numeric column type as it is a text. So we have no choice, but to load the data with the column type string, and later clean the data, and correct the data type.

Error during changing of the data type of the table

We continue our discussion of the preceding data load. After the data load is completed with the default data type, we clean the data in the CONTROL column using the following query:

```
Update thads2011 set CONTROL=substring(CONTROL,2,LEN(CONTROL)-2);
```

After correcting the data, we change the data type of the table thads2011 and column CONTROL to integer. However, we still get the error that we will have to drop and recreate the table. We can get the table creation script for the table thads2011 from SQL Server Management Studio, and create another table after changing the data type, and copy the data. If we are using any method that involves conversion or casting from one data type to another, care should be taken so that these types are compatible. The article at http://msdn.microsoft.com/en-us/library/ms187928.aspx shows the conversions that are allowed between different data types in SQL.

Troubleshooting the data mining structure performance

There can be many reasons why this might happen; in our case, if we make all the columns as input and try to generate the data mining structure, it will definitely take a long time because there will be a large number of trees or clusters to be generated depending on the algorithm that we are using. We will discuss a few of the commonly used algorithms and the parameters that can be altered to improve the processing performance.

The Decision Tree algorithm

The information that is required to classify data will proportionately increase with the increase in the input values. Therefore, there is a need to optimize the performance. The performance can be optimized by the following aspects:

- Reducing the number of inputs
- While grouping the items into bins, group only those values that provide the maximum information

We want to reduce the tree growth while trying not to lose the consistency and accuracy of the model. The following parameters help us to optimize the processing performance of the Decision Tree algorithm:

- COMPLEXITY_PENALTY: This parameter has a direct correlation to the tree growth. A lower value will increase the number of splits, while a higher number will reduce the number of splits.

- MINIMUM_SUPPORT: This parameter controls the minimum number of leaf cases required to generate a split in the Decision Tree algorithm. If this parameter is kept too small, there is a tendency of the algorithm to become overtrained and lose its capability to be generalized to other datasets. The default value is 10.

The Decision Tree algorithm will generate a new node each time the value of an attribute is found to be significantly correlated with the outcome. So, it is advisable to restrict the number of distinct values of an attribute. The article at http://msdn.microsoft.com/en-us/library/cc645868.aspx describes the factor affecting the growth of the model in more detail.

The Naïve Bayes algorithm

As discussed in *Chapter 5, Classification Models*, the Naïve Bayes algorithm is the least resource intensive algorithm and is more helpful in determining the initial trend of the data. The algorithm calculates the probability of each state of the input column when each state of the output column is provided. We can see this in Naïve Bayes Viewer of the model as discussed in *Chapter 5, Classification Models*, as shown in the following screenshot:

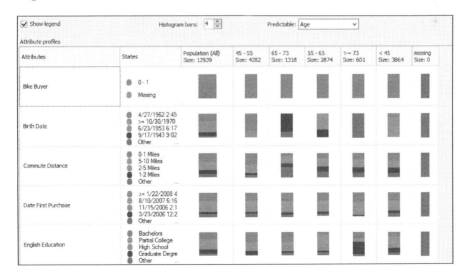

The three parameters that govern the processing performance of the algorithm are as follows:

- MAXIMUM_INPUT_ATTRIBUTES: With a default value of 255, the value of this parameter is the maximum number of input attributes that the algorithm can handle without invoking a feature selection. We can set this value to 0 to disable the feature selection.

- MAXIMUM_OUTPUT_ATTRIBUTES: With a default value of 255, the value of this parameter is the maximum number of output attributes that the algorithm can handle without invoking a feature selection. We can set this value to 0 to disable the feature selection.

- MINIMUM_STATES: This is the maximum number of states of the attribute that the algorithm can support. Beyond this, the algorithm will choose the most popular state and consider the remaining states as missing.

The Microsoft Clustering algorithm

The Microsoft Clustering algorithm works by grouping the cases that are present in the datasets into clusters that have similar characteristics. We visited the Microsoft Clustering algorithm in detail in *Chapter 6, Segmentation and Association Models*, and the following screenshot shows the model view that we generated:

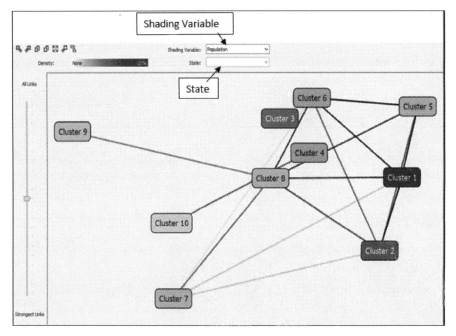

Segmentation Model revisited

The three aspects that will have an effect on the performance of this algorithm are as follows:

- Clustering technique
- Putting a limit to the maximum number of clusters
- Changing the support required to build a cluster

The parameters that will help us alter the preceding behavior are as follows:

- CLUSTERING_METHOD: This parameter specifies the clustering method that will be used. The available values are as follows:
    - Scalable EM
    - Non-scalable EM
    - Scalable K-means
    - Non-scalable K-means

    The default method is scalable EM, but we can use the non-scalable EM version to generate accurate models. Also, the memory requirement for scalable EM can be huge in case of large datasets. The scalable EM is faster. We can decide on the clustering method based on the amount of data and the resources available.

- CLUSTER_COUNT: This parameter represents the approximate number of clusters to be built by the algorithm. If the approximate number of clusters cannot be built from the data, the algorithm builds as many clusters as possible.

- MINIMUM_SUPPORT: This parameter specifies the minimum number of cases that are required to build a cluster. If the number of cases in the cluster is lower than this number, the cluster is treated as empty and discarded. So, setting this value too high might lead to discarding some valid clusters.

- MODELLING_CARDINALITY: This parameter specifies the number of sample models that are constructed during the clustering process. Reducing these numbers might increase the chances of losing out on some valid models.

- MAXIMUM_INPUT_ATTRIBUTES: This parameter specifies the maximum number of input attributes that the algorithm can handle before invoking the feature selection. Increasing the value of this parameter will degrade the performance.

- MAXIMUM_STATES: This parameter specifies the maximum number of attribute states that the algorithm supports. Increasing this value will degrade the performance.

Thus, we see that there are quite a few parameters that will affect the performance of the clustering model. The article at `http://msdn.microsoft.com/en-us/library/cc280445.aspx` provides more details about these parameters.

The Microsoft Association algorithm

The Microsoft Association algorithm works by traversing a dataset to find the items that appear together in a case. The algorithm will then group the associated items into itemsets that will appear, at a minimum, in the number of cases that are specified by the `MINIMUM_SUPPORT` parameter. The following screenshot is the model view of the Association model that we discussed in *Chapter 6, Segmentation and Association Models*:

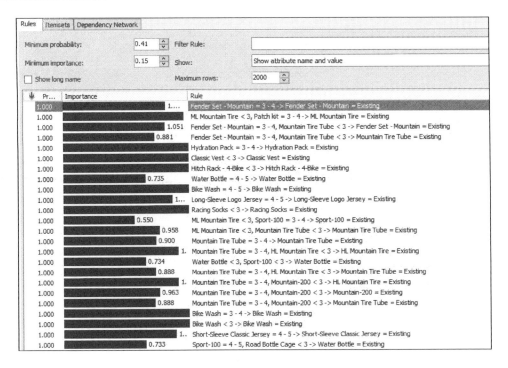

Looking at the preceding screenshot, it is quite obvious that the performance of the algorithm is mostly dependent on:

- The number of rules
- The maximum threshold to form an itemset
- The minimum threshold to form an itemset

The parameters that will help us control these three aspects are as follows:

- MAXIMUM_SUPPORT: This parameter helps filter out the items or cases that are too frequent in the dataset. Increasing the value of this parameter implies allowing more cases to be included, thereby increasing the chances of degraded performance.
- MINIMUM_SUPPORT: This parameter helps in eliminating the itemsets that are rare. While it might lead to a higher processing cost, it will improve the validity of the model.
- MINIMUM_PROBABILITY: This parameter helps in filtering out the rules with lesser possibility in the dataset. Increasing the value of this parameter might cause an overhead on the processing, but this increases the validity.

The article at `http://msdn.microsoft.com/en-us/library/cc280428.aspx` provides more information about the factors affecting the performance of the Microsoft Association algorithm.

The Microsoft Time Series algorithm

The Microsoft Time Series algorithm works by mixing the output of the **Autoregressive Integrated Moving Average Algorithm (ARIMA)** and **Autoregressive Tree Model for Time Series Analysis (ARTXP)** algorithms. The algorithm trains two separate models on the same dataset. One is based on the ARTXP dataset and the other is based on the ARIMA dataset. The predictions of the two models are then combined together to get the best prediction over various time slices. Over the initial period, the predictions of ARTXP are weighed more heavily, but as the time slice grows, the predictions of ARIMA begin to gain importance.

The following screenshot shows the Time Series graph of the model that we worked with in *Chapter 7, Sequence and Regression Models*:

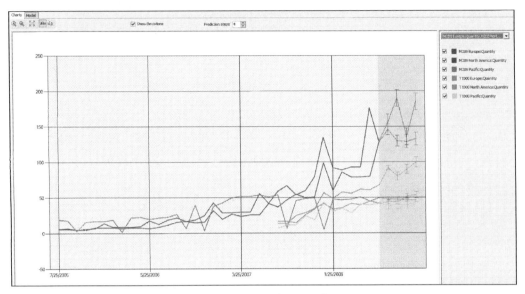

Time Series Graph revisited

We now know that there are two models that are generated by default and both of them can detect the periodicity of data. Some of the factors that impact the performance of the model are as follows:

- COMPLEXITY_PENALTY: This parameter controls the growth of the decision tree; decreasing this value will increase the chances of splits and degrade the performance
- MINIMUM_SUPPORT: This parameter controls the minimum time slices required to generate a split

The article at `http://msdn.microsoft.com/en-us/library/ms174923.aspx` gives more information on the factors affecting the performance of the algorithm.

Error during the deployment of a model

When deploying a model in *Chapter 9*, *Tuning the Models*, we got the following error:

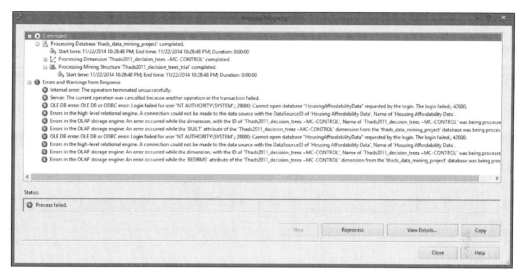

Error during deployment of the Model

The error states that the access to the `HousingAffordabilityData` database is not available to the user `NT Authority\SYSTEM`. The only place where the connection information is provided in a solution is in the **Data Source Impersonation** dialog box. So, we navigate to the **Impersonation Information** tab and check whether we have selected the **Use the service account** option, as shown in the following screenshot:

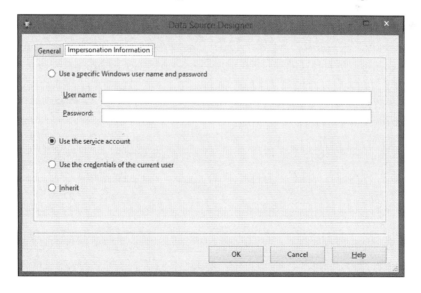

The article at `http://msdn.microsoft.com/en-us/library/ms187597.aspx` provides more information on each of the preceding options. The service account of the Analysis Services is shown in the following screenshot of the SQL Server Configuration Manager:

Name	State	Start Mode	Log On As	Process ID	Service Type
SQL Server Integration Services 11.0	Running	Manual	NT AUTHORITY\NETWORKSERVICE	5916	
SQL Server (MSSQLSERVER)	Running	Manual	LocalSystem	10976	SQL Server
SQL Server Analysis Services (MSSQLSERVER)	Running	Manual	LocalSystem	10428	Analysis Server
SQL Server Reporting Services (MSSQLSERVER)	Running	Manual	NT AUTHORITY\NETWORKSERVICE	5500	Report Server
SQL Server Browser	Running	Manual	NT AUTHORITY\LOCALSERVICE	9052	
SQL Server Agent (MSSQLSERVER)	Running	Manual	NT AUTHORITY\NETWORKSERVICE	5232	SQL Agent

We now navigate to the SQL Server Management Studio and check the permission of the user `LocalSystem` on the database `HousingAffordabilityData`, as shown in the following screenshot:

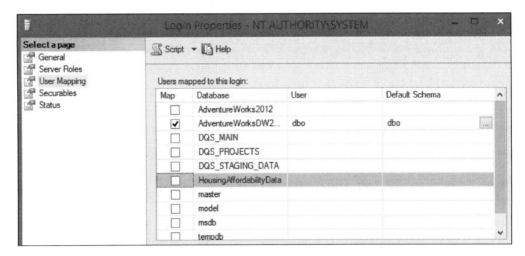

We can clearly see that the user does not have access to the database. We tick the checkbox and provide the user data reader privileges as we only need to read the data from the database. The model deployment is completed successfully in the next processing.

Summary

This chapter dealt with some of the technical problems that were encountered while working with the models throughout this book. While processing and deploying the models, the amount of data and the way in which the data is processed directly affects the time to deploy a solution. It also affects the accuracy of the models; we might also miss out on valid models if we do not tune the algorithm with the help of certain parameters. Therefore, we visited the models discussed in this book. We also discussed which parameters can be altered to improve the processing performance, ensuring the validity of the models. Lastly, we discussed the problem that we encountered during the deployment of the model and took corrective actions.

Index

Thank you for buying
Mastering SQL Server 2014 Data Mining

About Packt Publishing

Packt, pronounced 'packed', published its first book, *Mastering phpMyAdmin for Effective MySQL Management*, in April 2004, and subsequently continued to specialize in publishing highly focused books on specific technologies and solutions.

Our books and publications share the experiences of your fellow IT professionals in adapting and customizing today's systems, applications, and frameworks. Our solution-based books give you the knowledge and power to customize the software and technologies you're using to get the job done. Packt books are more specific and less general than the IT books you have seen in the past. Our unique business model allows us to bring you more focused information, giving you more of what you need to know, and less of what you don't.

Packt is a modern yet unique publishing company that focuses on producing quality, cutting-edge books for communities of developers, administrators, and newbies alike. For more information, please visit our website at www.packtpub.com.

About Packt Enterprise

In 2010, Packt launched two new brands, Packt Enterprise and Packt Open Source, in order to continue its focus on specialization. This book is part of the Packt Enterprise brand, home to books published on enterprise software – software created by major vendors, including (but not limited to) IBM, Microsoft, and Oracle, often for use in other corporations. Its titles will offer information relevant to a range of users of this software, including administrators, developers, architects, and end users.

Writing for Packt

We welcome all inquiries from people who are interested in authoring. Book proposals should be sent to author@packtpub.com. If your book idea is still at an early stage and you would like to discuss it first before writing a formal book proposal, then please contact us; one of our commissioning editors will get in touch with you.

We're not just looking for published authors; if you have strong technical skills but no writing experience, our experienced editors can help you develop a writing career, or simply get some additional reward for your expertise.

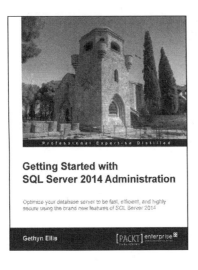

Getting Started with SQL Server 2014 Administration

ISBN: 978-1-78217-241-3   Paperback: 106 pages

Optimize your database server to be fast, efficient, and highly secure using the brand new features of SQL Server 2014

1. Design your SQL Server 2014 infrastructure by combining both on-premise and Windows Azure-based technology.

2. Implement the new InMemory OLTP database engine feature to enhance the performance of your transaction databases.

3. This is a hands-on tutorial that explores the new features of SQL Server 2014 along with giving real-world examples.

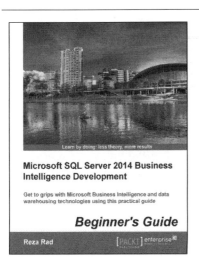

Microsoft SQL Server 2014 Business Intelligence Development Beginner's Guide

ISBN: 978-1-84968-888-8   Paperback: 350 pages

Get to grips with Microsoft Business Intelligence and data warehousing technologies using this practical guide

1. Discover the Dimensional Modeling concept while designing a data warehouse.

2. Learn Data Movement based on technologies such as SSIS, MDS, and DQS.

3. Design dashboards and reports with Microsoft BI technologies.

Please check **www.PacktPub.com** for information on our titles

Mastering Kali Linux for Advanced Penetration Testing

ISBN: 978-1-78216-312-1   Paperback: 356 pages

A practical guide to testing your network's security with Kali Linux, the preferred choice of penetration testers and hackers

1. Conduct realistic and effective security tests on your network.

2. Demonstrate how key data systems are stealthily exploited, and learn how to identify attacks against your own systems.

3. Use hands-on techniques to take advantage of Kali Linux, the open source framework of security tools.

Exploring Data with RapidMiner

ISBN: 978-1-78216-933-8   Paperback: 162 pages

Explore, understand, and prepare real data using RapidMiner's practical tips and tricks

1. See how to import, parse, and structure your data quickly and effectively.

2. Understand the visualization possibilities and be inspired to use these with your own data.

3. Structured in a modular way to adhere to standard industry processes.

Please check **www.PacktPub.com** for information on our titles